T0114656

# INFINITE AWAKENINGS

52 PHILOSOPHICAL STORY POEMS
ENVISIONING A MORE GLORIOUS WORLD

# OMAN KEN

BALBOA.PRESS
A DIVISION OF HAY HOUSE

Balboa Press books may be ordered through booksellers or by contacting:

Balboa Press
A Division of Hay House
1663 Liberty Drive
Bloomington, IN 47403
www.balboapress.com
844-682-1282

Print information available on the last page.

ISBN: 979-8-7652-3895-0 (sc)
ISBN: 979-8-7652-3896-7 (e)

Balboa Press rev. date: 04/24/2023

# ✳ CONTENTS ✳

The artistic expressions of dance, painting, music, poetry, and other art forms,
or the urge to create architectural masterpieces, or to climb a majestic mountain,
contain no important function that supports and benefits
the inborn drive regarding our instinctual physical survival.

These creative expressions are not fundamentally necessary for our survival,
yet we produce them in response to a natural innate impulse
that drives us forward toward our pursuit for the good and the beautiful,
our expanded connection with what really matters, greater service to others,
and a ceaseless inner longing to fully love all of life.

# ✳ DEDICATION ✳

This book is dedicated to
the creative and curious person
within us all
who is naturally inquiring
into what life is truly about
and what really matters.

Poetry helps bring meaning to our lives,
helps us be free thinkers,
and helps us navigate new perspectives
of how we look at the world
and our relationship to it.

# ✳ INTRODUCTION – THE GREAT STORY OF AWAKENING ✳

WHAT INSIGHTS AND REVELATIONS might a person receive when pondering what life is truly about? Could it be possible that the "job description" for every human being on the planet is to share their unique creative gifts and talents in ways that contribute to the lives of others? Doesn't it seem that this is the most natural thing in the world? For when scientists employ the inventions of massive telescopes or electron microscopes to genuinely examine our material reality - they discover there is a natural creativity at the foundation of all terrestrial phenomena and all systems throughout the Universe.

Everything in the world of Nature, from the largest scale to the smallest, is innately creative - and is in a constant process of exploring the unlimited potential of its creativity. For 13.8 billion years of perpetual unfolding, the Universe has been utilizing this infinite creativity to gradually manifest ever more order, diversity, innovation, and cooperation. This is called evolution - and you and I are small, but integral parts of this universal evolution through our participation in contributing our unique expressions of personal creativity that we share with the people around us.

Throughout my life I've always expressed my creativity in myriad ways, first drawing cartoons and comic books when I was a child, teaching myself to play electric guitar when I was a teenager, writing lots of songs and lyrics, designing and performing musical shows of ritual theater, orchestrating elaborate group celebrations of the solstices and equinoxes, and celebrating the wild dancer in me whenever I could.

Another creative expression I have enjoyed most of my adult life is writing poetry. I write most of my poetry when I am out exploring the wonders of nature, away from the daily patterns of my home life. I have dabbled with poetic expressions for decades and have written hundreds of rhyme-based lyrics for songs. Yet for years as I was spending time in Nature at the beautiful Oak Creek in Sedona, Arizona - and camping three to four times a year with a dear friend, I developed the primary themes for my four volume book series, **Journey of The Great Circle**.

During this period, my poetry took a whole new creative direction. I began to use my poetry to investigate the primary themes of personal and collective transformation that I was expressing within my book series. These themes dealt with spiritual awakening, inner freedom, the evolutionary perspective, existential paradox, self-love, and a host of other philosophical concepts. I would use my poetic expressions to tell stories that captured the essence or feeling tone of these ideas. Thus, I call my poetic adventures: philosophical story poems.

## The Natural Art of Story Making

At some unknown point in time, long after the initial utterances of primitive human speech that was spawned during the dawn of language, there emerged the very first appearance of an early mythic storyteller who would share symbolic tales with his small migrating tribe. These simple ancient stories were used to inspire and teach the younger ones in their group, and to point the inquisitive minds of their listeners toward the sacred place within them where they might envision a more effective way to survive - and eventually, to imagine a greater possibility for the future of their lives.

The elders of the tribe would tell stories of "the hero's journey", the essential inner journey of personal transformation that everyone must embark on, in order to one day develop more of their innate potential. Many thousands of years ago, these mythic storytellers originally shared their tales around blazing campfires under a star-strung sky. But then in time, as humanity evolved over countless eons, their inspiring sagas were brought indoors and expressed next to warm hearths within simple small cottages, which eventually, morphed into spacious modern living rooms.

At some point their stories were written down in books, and ultimately, acted out on medieval and present-day theatrical stages, then revealed on the screens of contemporary movie theaters, and now of course, are heard in various venues across the Internet. The thematic content of a good symbolic story has the potential to point us to our deepest and innermost connections with various aspects of reality, with a greater understanding of our relationship with life, and with a more intimate communion with the people and environment around us.

The numerous religious traditions of the world have referred to this fundamental mythic story or "hero's journey" - as *the spiritual journey*. Or in other words, the epic human *journey of awakening*. From the greater part of global mythic literature, this appears to be everyone's common story, for it is The Great Story of humanity's ongoing unfoldment of life **infinitely awakening.** *The journey of awakening* for all of humanity is the journey from unconsciousness to self-realization, from ignorance to enlightenment. It is the ceaseless progression of hearts and minds that are learning and developing into their fullest potential.

Every day we all tell ourselves some kind of story about who and what we believe we are, and what we think our relationship is with the world around us. Making up an everyday story about ourselves is a natural human endeavor that can beneficially serve our overall wellbeing. That is - if our personal story is constructive and empowering - and if we don't rigidly hold onto our personal story as some kind of absolute truth, believing it to be unchanging and static. The story of who and what we believe we are, which we inwardly tell ourselves daily, is always in a state of constant change, adaptation, and evolution. Our story will serve us well if we can utilize it to continually learn to patiently flow with, and embrace with responsibility, the perpetual changes within our life.

In order for our personal story to flourish, it's also beneficial for us to gain ever new and larger perspectives of who we believe we are, so we may continue to grow and expand our awareness of ourselves and our relationship to the world. We might say that our "common job description" - in other words, our purpose, meaning, and mission as conscious self-reflective humans - is to create the most life-affirming, productive, and evolutionary-supporting story that we can imagine. This kind of story will help to bring a more glorious world into form for one another - and for future generations. Through this self-reflective process, we eventually discover we can keep on reaching for the next horizon of possibility, so as to share the next higher version of our story with ourselves - and with others.

## A New Paradigm For Our Human Story

This book of story-poems speaks to the next level of our human story of awakening as I presently perceive and understand it, recognizing that our human story is constantly in a process of change and evolution. Humanity is now in the emerging process of awakening to its next expanded stage of consciousness. Each one of us has the possibility and responsibility to develop our fullest potential as part of this awakening, and to contribute our unique creative gifts and talents for the benefit of others.

There is so much more to life than meets the eye. Our modern culture is moving beyond the old paradigm defined by Newtonian physics and materialism that dominated the 20<sup>th</sup> century. Fortunately, many people are now opening their minds and hearts to the awareness of a new paradigm that includes quantum physics and transcendent paradox - where the role of consciousness and inner development is recognized and integrated into our 21st century thinking. This has profound implications for our personal lives - and how we can live collectively in a whole new harmonious manner.

We seem to be here on Earth in order to learn how to master the many aspects of our life, and to learn to love more fully, while compassionately serving one another. In other words - we are here to live "our personal creative story" which proclaims that we're part of an ever-evolving creative adventure of learning to be Masters of Freedom - learning to live a life of inner freedom and peace of mind by cultivating life mastery.

Infinite Awakenings Image

The image above represents the perpetual evolution - or the constant "awakenings" - that naturally take place in every aspect of Nature symbolized by the diamond, the flower, the bird, and the human being. At one time, millions of years ago, there was only a plethora of green vegetation on the planet. The beautiful manifestation of flowers had not yet arrived on the evolutionary scene. But over time and with gradual development, evolving life eventually found a way to empower a brand-new emergent form to arise - the very first flower.

For the first flower to take shape on Earth, a radical shift in consciousness was required within the plant kingdom. This new expression of vegetative form could poetically be thought of as an "enlightenment" or "awakening" of the plant kingdom. A similar kind of radical shift in consciousness also occurred in the mineral kingdom with the first diamond - and later, in the animal kingdom with the first flight of a bird. The same expansive evolutionary impulses in consciousness are happening right now throughout the world as they continuously have from the beginning of the Universe. Each person on the planet is now, consciously or unconsciously, evolving and developing into his or her destiny as an awakened human.

## Why We Read Poetry

We typically don't read poetry for mere recreation. Poetry is read because of a desire to experience and feel the full spectrum of emotion and passion of what it means to be human. Poetry helps bring meaning to our lives, be free thinkers, and navigate new perspectives of how we look at the world and our relationship to it.

I like to think of these story poems as imaginations of what we can dream and envision for the future of our lives - and the future of the planet. With our deepest imaginings we can dream into physical form our new realities. We can utilize poetry to imagine the most novel and glorious expressions of beauty and goodness on Earth.

I also suggest that you read these story poems out loud. They are meant to be read out loud. There is an added power to the experience that can be viscerally felt when the words are expressed vocally. One way to do this is to read these story poems to a friend or Loved One.

## An Awakening Journey of Discovery

This book of story poems is called **Infinite Awakenings** because each of the poems are designed to point toward an awareness of *the awakening journey of discovery* that we are all being invited to experience. It also points to the understanding that every "individual awakening" which a person embodies in their life is part of "a vast endless spectrum of awakenings" that's perpetually taking place throughout the Universe.

During my life I have felt a deep connection to this *Infinite Creative Impulse* within me - especially when I am in Nature alone amidst the stillness. Within its wondrous silent sanctuaries are the places I experience more freedom to jot down my poems and write my deepest thoughts. It is this silence of the natural world that helps me access richer parts of my being.

My intention is that these story poems
will help you envision a more glorious world
for you, your family and community, and for the planet.
May they point you to a more expanded perspective
of what your life is truly about
and what really matters.

# 1

# PORTALS
# OF
# PERSPECTIVE

# Introduction to the Poem – *The Last Castle*

IN THE SUMMER OF 2010, I traveled through the forested towns of Germany where I was mesmerized by the timeworn stones of so many ancient walls and the ruins of castles. I could sense that the primal energy fields of these old stone walls contained diverse historical memories. They spoke to me regarding what we, as humanity, have lived through to develop human culture to our present day, which includes our sustained quest for cultivating democracy, global cooperation, and civilized inclusion.

Yet these massive walls were initially built with an intention to keep "the bad people" separated from "the good people" - "your people" segregated from "our people" - due to the fear and judgment that existed at the time. For millennia the strife of war, brutality of the powerful, greed of the elite, and ignorance of the masses have kept us humans from experiencing the deeper spiritual reality of our connection as one human family.

Just as it is taking a long time for these ancient walls and castles to deteriorate, it's also taking a long time for humanity to fully learn the collective lessons of love, forgiveness, compassion, and inclusion. This ongoing moral development has required thousands of years of trial and error - countless battles between the illusion of "good and evil" - to bring our world to where it is today.

Yet nowadays, the walls of separation that remain between certain groups of people are mostly barriers within individual hearts and minds, rather than the insulation of external walls. They are imaginary blockages consisting of a false self-image we think we need defend, our obsessive belief we need to be in control, our notion we need to gain the approval of others - as well as our habitual fear of the unknown.

This poem explores the constant invitation from *Life* to courageously journey within so as to finally, personally and collectively, learn to remove the walls.

✳    ✳    ✳    ✳

# Circle of the Young Awakening Self
## (Fear-based and Self-centered Strategies to Survive Emotionally)

**THE FEARFUL MIND**
WHEN I'M NOT ALIGNED,
I LIVE IN CONSTANT
FEAR OF THE UNKNOWN,
OF RELIVING THE PAST,
OF CONCERNS ABOUT
THE FUTURE - AND
ATTEMPT TO COVER UP
MY ANXIETY OF DEATH

**THE DEFENDER**
WHEN I'M NOT ALIGNED,
I IDENTIFY WHO I AM
AS SEPARATE FROM
OTHERS - THINKING I AM
MY BODY, MY FEELINGS,
MY THOUGHTS, "MY
STORIES", CREATING
A FALSE SELF-IMAGE
I BELIEVE I MUST DEFEND

**THE CONTROLLER**
WHEN I'M NOT ALIGNED,
I THINK I NEED TO BE
IN CONTROL AND GAIN
THE APPROVAL
OF OTHERS
IN ORDER TO ENSURE
THE CONTINUITY
OF MY SELF-IMAGE

**THE PROTECTER**
WHEN I'M NOT ALIGNED,
I NEED TO PROTECT MY
SELF-IMAGE FROM THE
ATTACKS AND OPINIONS
OF OTHERS BY BUILDING
WALLS OF SEPARATION
SO I CAN SURVIVE
EMOTIONALLY

# The Last Castle

Who carried the regal name
  Of the French king
    Or the German duke
      Or the monarch of England
        Whose crowning fate
          Was to erect the last castle?

That final majestic stone monolith
  With high impenetrable walls
    Of chiseled rock in gripping mortar
      That for a fleeting moment
        Restrained foreboding evil
          And the pounding darkness of a yonder world

The protected pinnacles shaped for survival
  Where mythic men could stand anchored
    Ready with brazen weapons and bloodstained armor
      Fashioned to fight invaders from the north
        Barbarians from the south
          And one's raging neighbors
            Beyond forested hills
              Whose only quest
                Was to pillage the innocent
                  And bath in another's river of treasures

Spanning early Victorian ages
  European royalty bargained with the gods
    To constrain the fainthearted
      To maintain dominion
        Built lavish strongholds of carved stone
          Sculpted rock walls to secure their hoards
            And tall cylindrical towers
              To know the hour of the trumpet
                And when to raise the sword

The rough-hewed walls of imperial castles
   Are no longer raised amidst crests and verdant hilltops
     For our new citadels have grown much too large
       Encompassing entire nations - worlds - and battling ideas

Now fortresses are glaringly constructed
   With the stones of crippled capitalism - crumbling socialism
   And unbridled nationalism
     Yet these unseen stones are firmly cemented in place
     With the same fear-laden mortar

We've built barbed curtains between East and West Berlin
   North and South Korea
     We raise blazing fences between Israel and Palestine
     Between the States and immigrants of Mexico
     And implicate the Great Wall of China
       As one of the revered monuments
         To the impediment of invasion

We lay barricades between Christians and Moslems
   Irish Catholics and Protestants - Aryans and Jews
     And any "other" - "they" or "them"
       Who happen to stride
         On the farther side
          Of the check point of hate

So many castles
   Built within the ruins of our minds
     Habitual thoughts - whose only propensity
       Is to raise barriers of separation
         Notions of an age-old terror invade us from the north
           The engrained impulses of possession and greed
         Attack like barbarians from the south
          And our raging neighbor-like hallucinations
        Of grasping for control
       Clinging to power
         Reign just over the hill of our awareness

Old fortresses of England - Germany - France - and Spain
  Are invigorating to inspect
    To explore the mystery of their crushed ruins
      To touch the eons humanity has anguished through

To help us acknowledge
  The epic journey we have all embarked on
    To sneak a glimpse
      Of where we might be headed
        To climb step by step to the apex
          Of a tall watchtower
            And ponder into today's horizon
              At the potential of sculpting
                An entirely new world

An exalted world where I can choose
  To cross the drawbridge
    So I may gaze into your eyes
      In some land where there are no castle walls
        No dividing barricades
          No plates of armor between us

For the day I sincerely recognize you
  Witnessing "us" and "them" forever melt
    Bravely staring into a mirror of my authentic self
      Is the day I ascend up the winding stairway
        Of an ancient tower no longer required
          And etch my name
            Into the disappearing stone
              Where I must then leap into the unknown

The prescient void where I know with certitude
  My generation of forging walls is over
    For I have built my last castle

✻

✻ · ✻

✻

# Introduction to the Poem - _A Very Fortunate Sailor_

THIS POEM WAS INSPIRED BY one of the Contemplation Circles from the Winter Volume of **Journey of _The Great Circle_**. It is called "An Ocean Journey - a Metaphor for _the Journey of Awakening_".

This Contemplation Circle explores the idea that life is _a journey of endless discovery, a journey of self-mastery, a spiritual journey._ It is a transformative journey of ever-expansive learning and inner development in which we, as individuals, naturally ascend or develop through ever-higher stages of awareness.

In this metaphoric story-poem, our quest - or hero's journey - begins in a stage of awareness in which we habitually believe in the illusion that we are a victim of life's difficulties and afflictions. As a helpless victim in a hostile world, it initially seems we have little or no control over them.

Yet eventually over time our awareness expands, based on what we discover from our diverse life experiences. We learn ever-greater perspectives of who we really are and, thus, begin to take more conscious responsibility for our life. As we do this, the vessel of our heart and mind becomes more evolved and more developed.

Each progressive vessel of experience that we become aware of allows us to move through the adventure of our life with more peace, harmony, and inner freedom. Ultimately, we discover there is nowhere to go - and nothing to do - except to be the magnificence of who we have always been.

✳    ✳    ✳    ✳

This poem is included in the **Autumn Volume** of **Journey of _The Great Circle_** by Oman Ken - a book of daily transformative practices.

# Circle of "An Ocean Journey"
## (A Metaphor for the *Journey of Awakening)*

**THE FULLY INTEGRATED LIFE**
KNOWING *"THE ONE"* WHO TRULY NAVIGATES THE SCHOONER, *"THE INNER CAPTAIN",* AND *"THE ONE WHO JOURNEYS UPON THE OCEAN"* HAVE ALWAYS BEEN ONE AND THE SAME

**THE UNEXAMINED LIFE**
ONE WHO DRIFTS UPON THE OCEAN OF LIFE ON A RAFT WITHOUT A SAIL OR RUDDER, AND IS HAPHAZARDLY TOSSED BY THE WIND AND WAVES

**THE SURRENDERED LIFE**
ONE WHO NAVIGATES THE OCEAN OF LIFE ON A MAJESTIC SCHOONER WHERE ALL COMMANDS COME FROM THE GUIDANCE OF *"AN INNER BENEVOLENT CAPTAIN"*

**THE SELF-REFLECTIVE LIFE**
ONE WHO NAVIGATES THE OCEAN OF LIFE ON A LARGE SAILBOAT, HAS CLARITY OF DIRECTION, AND ASKS MEANINGFUL QUESTIONS ON A SEARCH FOR WHAT IS TRUE

# A Very Fortunate Sailor

Once again - it was the perpetual sunrise of his life
He had faced a similar taste of dawn
A thousand times before
For *the Exalted Essence* of his being
Had fashioned for him
Myriad uncharted oceans
Where he might carry out his inquiries
His epic expeditions to explore
The limitless realms of enchantment
The places where the budding flower of his heart
Could blossom into more generous fields of glory
To reveal the jewel
Of what is genuine and unquestionable
Of that which never changes

Yet - during this precise morning of his endless voyage
His newborn eyes were still blinded
By the abject drudgery
And seeming havoc of a hostile world
His heavy heart still thickly veiled
In the unrelenting illusions reigning down
His busy mind still cluttered
With the meaningless pursuits of untamed desires

And then - once more
As he had done so many times before
He drifted without direction upon a vast ocean
Floating on his tiny raft without sail or rudder
Haphazardly being tossed by winds and waves
Mechanically thrown from one ripple to another
Until the long hard day of his life
Came to an unavoidable completion
At the caress of midnight

It required countless arduous eons
  Of aimlessly drifting upon his rudimentary crafts
    Time and time again
      Until finally he landed within a promised dawn of his life
        In which everything was by some means altered
          As if he was now looking out
            From a more elevated precipice upon the mountain
              Where his novel insights and broadened perspectives
                Invited him to embrace a more luscious reality
                  One that offered him
                    A superior way to journey forward

The paltry rudderless raft dissolved
  While his *Sublime Essence* sculpted yet another vessel
    A sea-worthy ship erected to navigate an immense ocean
      A finely constructed craft with large sails
        To seize the grandeur of the wind
          And a stable rudder to forge a calculated direction
            Like an arrow thrust towards its target
              Released from the bow of an unruffled heart

It was a range of probing questions about meaning
  His authentic inquiry into purpose
    The passionate search for life's greater story
      That positioned him behind the ship's helm
        Steering this majestic vessel
          Knowingly navigating its course
            Until the day of his life expired
              Into one more portal of midnight's silence

Yet again - sundry eons passed
  Until he found himself at an unparalleled morning of his life
    Where this time - his *Oceanic Heart* knew he was ready
      And thus patterned a majestic schooner
        With multiple masts of colossal sails
          Attached to wooden decks expertly crafted
            And highly ornamented with seasoned artistry

On this voyage he became skilled
  At surrendering his entire ship
    And all longstanding control
      To the benevolent commands of an *Inner Captain*
        To an *Ultimate Force*
          Orchestrating the ceaseless unfolding of the Cosmos
            To the *Intelligence* that ultimately commands all ships
              That persistently explore and chart
                The unending corners of existence

On this schooner - there was nowhere to go
  Yet he reached every distant shore amid perfect timing
    On this regal vessel - there was nothing to do
      Yet the world he sailed was becoming
        A more glorious sanctuary with each fleeting sunset

But just as all ships assemble their allotted time at sea
  And must one day revert to the eventual fate of dry dock
    This schooner too found its way back to the harbor
      From its wealth of revelations upon a boundless ocean
        And disappeared into the next threshold of midnight

It is a very fortunate sailor
  Who one day awakens to that destined dawning of life mastery
    Who recognizes that *Life* perfectly navigates life
      That *"The One"* who truly pilots the schooner
        And the *"Inner Captain"*
          As well as the *"Journeyer upon the Ocean"*
            Are now - and have always been - one and the same

Then and there - he watched himself
  Begin to share with others
    The saga of his epic adventure
      Declaring that as every sailor
        First embarks upon their ocean odyssey
          They may initially believe they need to steer the ship
            But in reality - all they need do is enjoy the ride

# Introduction to the Poem – _The Puzzle Piece_

A PICTURE JIGSAW PUZZLE is a creative exercise of putting together hundreds, sometimes thousands, of unique separate pieces of a picture that interlock together to form one complete image. Of course, all the individual puzzle pieces are necessary if one wants to experience the finished picture in its entirety. Many people use picture puzzles to relax and quiet the mind - or as a way to have fun.

This poem is an exploration into how each of us is a unique expression of the vast creativity of the Universe. It also explores the idea that our creative gifts and talents are meant to be offered in service to the people in our life. Every one of us is an important and integral part of the Big Picture of _All That Is_ - and life would be missing a unique piece if we weren't alive to share our personal gifts.

The poem investigates the notion that we all possess a novel point-of-view - a personal vantage, which is absolutely correct and true for us, based on how we uniquely perceive reality. Yet we must remember it's only a partial perspective of the whole.

For example, we may hold an exterior perspective to some situation (such as - climate change is causing lots of disastrous climate dilemmas and political legislation needs to be enacted to encourage people to change the way they live) - yet for others, there's an interior perspective to be considered as well (such as - some people are in the habit of their current lifestyles and find it complicated to change the way they live). We may understand an individual perspective about some relationship issue (a person may want to drive their car as fast as they desire) - yet there's also a collective perspective to be taken into account (the safety of the community).

Therefore, to experience the greatest peace and harmony with others, we require all of our various perspectives so as to mutually comprehend the entire picture of what's really happening and needed in any given moment.

※　　※　　※　　※

# Circle of Fundamental Universal Perspectives
## (Four Vantages of Every Life Form, Challenge, or Opportunity)

**INDIVIDUAL**
A PERSPECTIVE THAT
DEFINES A SINGULAR
EXPRESSION OF A CERTAIN
SPECIES OF LIFE,
A SINGLE CATEGORY OF
PHYSICAL STRUCTURES,
OR A DISTINCT ANIMAL
OR PERSON

**INTERIOR**
A PERSPECTIVE THAT
DEFINES A YEARNING
TO EXPAND AWARENESS,
LEARN WHAT IS TRUE,
AND DEVELOP POTENTIAL
- AND DESCRIBES
THE INTERNAL WORLD
OF MIND AND HEART

**EXTERIOR**
A PERSPECTIVE THAT
DEFINES A YEARNING
TO CREATE, EXPRESS
GREATER DIVERSITY, AND
CONTRIBUTE ONE'S GIFTS
- AND RELATES TO ONE'S
BODY, ENVIRONMENT,
NATURE, THE UNIVERSE

**COLLECTIVE**
A PERSPECTIVE THAT
DEFINES HAVING
A RELATIONSHIP
WITH, AND BEING
AN INTEGRAL PART OF,
A LARGER GROUP OF
LIFE - SUCH AS A FAMILY,
GROUP OR NATION

# The Puzzle Piece

She labored arduously for the past six days
    Struggling to complete a 200-piece picture puzzle
      Which lay affixed to her dining room table
        Illustrating the profoundly striking telescopic photo
          Of the Andromeda Nebula

She sensed a crushing ache of defeat sink into her
    As she approached the closing turn of the contest
      Only to establish one piece missing
        Creating an obvious vacancy
          Near the heart of the astronomic icon

Of course each puzzle piece is indispensible
    Yet the absent piece screamed out
      It was the most essential of all
        For without it - there loomed a torrential hole in her *Soul*

Every solitary piece of a puzzle is unique
    Comprising its own novel shapes - contours - and stabs of color
      Some are liberal Democrats
        And some are conservative Republicans
        Some are fundamentalist Christians
        Or monastic Hindus
          Or Moslems - Jews - Sufis - Taoists - or Atheists

Some are movie celebrities
    While others are simple laborers
      Some have lofty philosophies to change the world
        Yet others live in a self-made tiny box with hardly a notion

Each piece has its own slant of absorbing reality
    Its own exclusive perspective on the advance of life
    Its own vantage of how things are moving along
    Its own position within this multilayered world

It's amusing how every point of view is always accurate
How every style of examining reality is absolutely correct
That is  - when you're witnessing the common verses of life
From the supreme center of the Cosmos

Yet each distinctive perspective is but a partial one
Only an incomplete assessment
Of monitoring the entire scene

So to garner the unabridged picture with all its magnificence
We're urged to view it from every possible angle
From the unparalleled vantage
Of each and every puzzle piece

All pieces of the puzzle bear their own gift
Hold a superior treasure to offer this tender world
Cradle their unique blessings to donate to the mix
Whether large and impressive
Or small and inconspicuous

Puzzle pieces are meant to merge intimately
To precisely interlock into a tapestry of contour
To help produce a well-defined image of the entire display

They are designed to entangle one another
To bring about a more beautiful coalescence
Than can be achieved by just a solitary piece

They long to be communal - cooperative
An integral part of the clan
To be one with the tribe

She stared into the gaping hole
Into the saddened heart of the puzzle
For what tasted like an eternity
The missing fragment of the Andromeda Nebula
That stirred a despondency in her *Soul*

She had known this void countless times before
  It had become tirelessly habitual
    Yet for a nameless reason
      The shadowy abyss now spoke to her
        She noticed its emptiness was gone

Suddenly she realized
  The moment had finally come
    Time to stop assembling
      One picture puzzle after the next
        Sitting all alone at her dining room table
        Season after season
        Year after year
          Tear after tear

Somehow she boldly stood up
  Put on her red dancing dress
    Adorned her face to greet a new world
      Courageously opened the door
        And stepped out into the starry heavens
        Offering her unique puzzle piece
        To a desirous Universe
          Which easily slipped into the hole
          That waited to be filled
            In a way only she could fill

✳

✳ · ✳

✳

# Introduction to the Poem – *The Glass Telescope*

MODERN SCIENCE HAS GIVEN US TOOLS to discover the natural patterns and forms of order within Nature that shape and define our understanding of the world around us. Two of the most powerful instruments of science for investigating many of the wonders within our world and the Universe - are the telescope - and the microscope.

A powerful telescope can give us greater comprehension of what is taking place in the far reaches of the Cosmos. The microscope can reveal to us more of the mesmerizing world of biological molecules and minute particles within the living world.

This poem explores how the natural patterns and phenomena within the Universe, both at a telescopic scale - as well as a microscopic scale, seem to have many similarities. For example, the intelligent patterns of massive solar systems throughout our galaxy look like infinitesimally small patterns of orbiting electrons around a central nucleus. And the celestial patterns of distant stars look like miniscule patterns of cells within the body of a living organism.

The poem also points us to a recognition of our Oneness - our Unity with all things. Metaphysically, it has been stated that when we're observing any finite aspect of the Universe, we are looking at an aspect of ourselves. Sounds like a real stretch - but is it?

✳    ✳    ✳    ✳

# Circle of the Fractal Nature of Emergent Evolution
## (In Relation to the Awakening Human)

**THE EVOLUTION OF PLANET EARTH**
THE EARTH, AS WELL AS OUR ENTIRE SOLAR SYSTEM, EVOLVED FROM A MASSIVE SUPERNOVA AND, OVER TIME, THE EARTH *AWAKENED* INTO A LIVING ORGANISM

**THE EVOLUTION OF THE AWAKENED HUMAN**
MODERN HUMANS ARE EVOLVING TOWARD NEW EMERGENT STAGES OF *AWAKENING*, REPEATING THE FRACTAL PATTERNS OF ALL LIVING SYSTEMS

**THE EVOLUTION OF EARLY HUMANS**
PRIMITIVE HUMANS EVOLVED FROM THE EARLY BIOLOGICAL LIFE OF PLANET EARTH, REPEATING A SIMILAR FRACTAL PATTERN OF EMERGENT *AWAKENING*

**THE EVOLUTION OF THE SELF-REFLECTIVE MIND**
THE HUMAN MIND EVOLVED AND BECAME SELF-REFLECTIVE, *AWAKENING* ANOTHER REPEATING EMERGENT FRACTAL PATTERN

# The Glass Telescope

He was a very inquisitive little man
  Yet he felt huge
    Every time he gazed long into the midnight sky
      Surveying through the polished eyepiece
        Of his gigantic telescope
          Nestled high above the low-lying clouds
            Atop an idyllic mountain vista

He searched endlessly for simple answers
  To the Big Questions
    There - within this colossal sculpture of steel and glass
      He felt as if he could reach out his hand
        Touch the rings of Saturn
          And neighboring spectral planets
            Whirling like orbiting electrons

With a swift calculated adjustment
  There emerged another solar system to spy
    With jeweled starlight shimmering at its core
      Radiating like a solar nucleus
        The hub of a cosmic wheel

Turning the mammoth instrument a bit more
  He observed a million points of luminance
    Star clusters singing in concert
      Throughout an adjacent galaxy
        Like whirling particles within a single atom

His telescope extended absurdly deep
  Into the endless corners of the Cosmos
    Viewing the spiral etchings of far-flung galaxies
      Each a silvery bead upon the necklace of God
        Celestial cells within the ubiquitous body of creation

Then myriad clusters of outlying galaxies
    Making up a tapestry of molecules
        The further artistry of jewels
            In a monumental star-strung heaven

With his scope stretching to its severe limits
    Glimpsing as far as he possibly could
        Suddenly - the little man
            Gazed into the soul of a titanic enigma
            One he never could have imagined

There - at the sheer edge of the Cosmos
    Was a colossal gigantic man
        With one eye gazing into an enormous microscope
        Enchanted and dazzled
            By every miniscule feature there was to behold

The gigantic man peered into the microscope
    Examining a single drop of his own blood
        A scarlet jewel containing an unfathomable Universe
        Of boundless energy and motion
            Within its spatial boundaries

He observed minute plasma molecules
    Viewing infinitesimal swirling clusters
        That spun like torroidal galaxies

Zooming closer
    Into the matrix of atomic particles
        He surveyed a parade of cells
            As if he were peering
                Into the Milky Way's endless starry belt

Pulsing biotic cells were comprised
    Of innumerable atoms
        Which shone like countless star clusters
            Magnetized together by an invisible core

At the kernel of each atom
His eyes dove into a fiery nucleus
Like the heartbeat
Of an intricately designed solar system

Churning around this luminous nucleus
Danced orbiting electrons of multi-hued patterns
While his eye converged on a solitary one
Which offered a common appearance
Of some white and blue pearl
Floating through oceans of endless space

Then - as the gigantic man focused his microscope in closer
His breath abruptly stopped in a moment of sublime amazement
As he became suspended in a conundrum
That utterly shivered his world

A realization of exalted wonder
For he was looking at a very little man
Who was standing on a white and blue pearl
With one eye staring into a gigantic telescope
Which was gazing right back at him

At the same instant - their two eyes collided
The tender fabric of the Universe ripped open
The gash revealed a portal of paradox
Leading within and beyond all time and space

Looking outward germinates the seeds
Of gratitude and surrender
Looking inward inspires the harvest
Of acceptance and the awakening of oneness

Questioning everything creates wondrous new worlds
Contemplation opens up novel vistas and perspectives
The essential inquiry into who we really are
Blessing us with unimaginable treasures

At the moment of this unfathomable glimpse of communion
   The little man looked into his gigantic telescope
      And noticed
         He was gazing into a perfect mirror

The gigantic man peered into his little microscope
   And became aware
      He also - was gazing into a deified mirror

The little man and the gigantic man
   Exploded - with the astute realization
      That all this time
         They were simply looking at themselves
           And it was good

# Introduction to the Poem – _Parallel Universes_

THERE IS A THEORY IN QUANTUM PHYSICS which states that the reality we call "our life" may be experienced through multiple realms of parallel universes. A parallel universe can be described as a universe that's different than our own which exists within some other dimension of reality. This "other universe" is taking place simultaneously with our current experience of the known universe. In fact, some theories, based on advanced mathematics, suggest there are many parallel universes that are possible to experience. And there may even be an infinite number of parallel universes which exist.

Some progressive theorists have speculated that it's the specific focus of our conscious awareness that determines which of these parallel universes we will experience at any given moment. Of course, this is a pretty far-out notion based on what we experience in our everyday reality. But who knows - it may be true!

This poem was inspired by this expansive concept from quantum physics - and by the idea that each of us is mentally and emotionally creating the unique "story" of our lives in every moment. Every day we live out the creation of our personal "story" based on our current belief systems - and the focused attention of our awareness. Could it be that if we could learn to change our life story, alter our belief systems, and refocus our conscious awareness, we could begin living in a parallel universe with a completely different outcome?

\*　　\*　　\*　　\*

# Circle of the Visionary Storyteller
## (An Archetype of Conscious Contribution)

**SHARE INSPIRATION**
I SHARE "STORIES"
THAT INSPIRE PEOPLE
TO DEVELOP
THEIR POTENTIAL
AND CONTRIBUTE THEIR
CREATIVE GIFTS TO THE
WELLBEING OF OTHERS

**DEVELOP
AWARENESS**
I TELL "STORIES"
THAT ASSIST OTHERS
TO DEVELOP
HIGHER AWARENESS
AND CULTIVATE
A DEEPER MEANING
AND PURPOSE OF LIFE

**INCLUSIVE
PERSPECTIVES**
I EXPRESS "STORIES"
THAT EMPOWER OTHERS
TO EMBRACE LIFE
WITH MORE INCLUSIVE
PERSPECTIVES
OF WHAT REALLY
MATTERS

**CELEBRATE
LIFE**
I DO WHAT I CAN TO SERVE
OTHERS BY OFFERING
"STORIES" THAT ARE
EMPOWERING, UPLIFTING,
AND WHICH CELEBRATE
THE MANY GLORIOUS
FACETS OF LIFE

# Parallel Universes

After numerous fruitful decades
  Or maybe copious fertile lifetimes
    Of arduous incremental ascent
      Navigating the meandering upward path
        That directs all seekers to the Throne of Light
          She realized she was - at last - triumphantly standing
          At the crest of the mountain once again

Or at least - it seemed the apparent peak
  Of yet another of the journey's endless summits
    A lofty place of sanctity and freedom
      Where she could easily gaze out
        Upon the 360-degree spectrum of infinite possibility
          And observe the diverse hues of creation
            The unlimited veils of parallel universes
              Which were all accessible on her horizon

By merely altering her head slightly
  Deliberately shifting her eyes faintly to the right - or left
    Towards a promising landscape she preferred to view
      She was free to boldly refocus her awareness
        Onto a whole new slice of existence
          From the countless opportunities offered her
            And fashioned her personal storyline
              Based on the changing streams
                Of her ever fluid - yet novel beliefs

She constantly improved her inner saga
  As each day she altered the movement of the tides
    With the flicker of a thought
      Around the mutable tale she told herself
        As if suddenly changing a TV channel
          To a more wondrous and illuminating way
            Of celebrating the magnificence of her Light

Or by her methodical calculations
    She jumped ahead into a future chapter
        Of the holy book of her life
            That eternally mirrors back to her
            And poetically reveals
                Her yet unclaimed potential

She is the mythic story maker
    Forever rewriting the supreme tale of her life
        She is the fabled scriptwriter
            Churning out diverse comic and dramatic scenes
                Which she is to act out
                    Upon the mutable stage of a million moments
                    She is the hallowed edgewalker
                        Pioneering the limitless uncharted territories
                        Of all that is humanly possible

Her exclusive story is ever malleable
    Ever transforming
        Shifting from one universe to another
            As she unwaveringly chooses
                A different twist in the narrative
                As she courageously declares
                    The transmutation of her parable
                    To an awakened saga
                        Of reverence and remembrance

So now - she again triumphantly
    Stands on the mountaintop
        And mindfully creates her day
            To be the absolute best story
                Her humble heart can imagine
                By keeping her central gaze
                In the clear direction
                    Of her most glorious tomorrows

# II

# JOURNEYS OF
## THE GREAT CIRCLE

# Introduction to the Poem - *The Diver*

IT WAS A SCORCHING JUNE OF 2008. I placed all of my camping gear into a canoe and headed down river into the wilderness. The morning winds were still and the river water reflected like a silvery mirror. A few echoes of birds sliced through the silence.

The idea for this poem came while I was in deep contemplation as the dawning sun was just rising over the silhouetted trees. There were jagged rock cliffs on the other bank of the river. I imagined that a man was standing on a rock precipice with a yearning to courageously dive into the cool waters below.

Then one of my Contemplation Circles came to mind regarding the foundational theme: Pillars of Awakening. These Pillars are qualities for cultivating inner freedom, a life of self-mastery. The four qualities depicted as the Pillars of Awakening are:

1) **Gratitude** - I am grateful for what I'm learning from every experience of my life.

2) **Surrender** - I let go of my attachments and surrender everything in my life to *a Greater Power*.

3) **Acceptance** - I accept that my life is unfolding perfectly just as it is.

4) **Oneness** - I am aware of my Oneness with all of life.

I imagined that the four unique stages of his dive from the rock ledge were portraying these four awakening qualities.

For many years, I have started my morning meditation by consciously connecting with these four pillars. Now as I bring them into my awareness each day, I sometimes visualize "the diver" as well.

✳   ✳   ✳   ✳

This poem is included in the **Summer Volume** of **Journey of The Great Circle** by Oman Ken - a book of daily transformative practices.

# Circle of the Pillars of Awakening
## (Attributes For Cultivating Inner Freedom and a Life of Mastery)

**ONENESS**
I AM AWARE
OF MY ONENESS
WITH ALL
OF LIFE

**GRATITUDE**
I AM GRATEFUL
FOR WHAT I'M LEARNING
FROM EVERY
EXPERIENCE OF MY LIFE

**ACCEPTANCE**
I ACCEPT
THAT MY LIFE IS
UNFOLDING PERFECTLY
JUST AS IT IS

**SURRENDER**
I LET GO
OF MY ATTACHMENTS
AND SURRENDER MY LIFE
TO *A GREATER POWER*

# The Diver

His bronze sculpted body stood suspended
　For what seemed an endless eternity
　　Both feet anchored
　　　At the edge of a high rock precipice
　　　　Overlooking the rippling waters of the sea below
　　　　His eyes gazing out in all directions

He patiently watched the slow turning of seasons
　The bitter cold biting at his skin
　　The soft blanket of air cradling him
　　　Storms - cyclones - and haunting whirlwinds
　　　And the glories of a perfect twilight

Finally he discovers his moment of absolute stillness
　The sanctified place where he revels
　　In whatever arises before him
　　　Giving thanks for how it shaped him
　　　　How it formed the curves of his body and mind
　　　　　Grateful for the wondrous gifts of every breath
　　　　　For the energy of aliveness pulsing through him

And now ready to proceed
　Taking a final step to the rim of the rocky cliff
　　Looking down at the churning water below
　　　The sight of a swirling emerald ocean
　　　Awakens an impulse of realization

His body prepares itself
　With a relaxed sigh of commitment
　　Adrenaline surging through the fibers of every muscle
　　　Bending knees in focused anticipation
　　　　Like a tiger perched to lunge on its prey

Then with an explosive vault
  He catapults himself forward
    Leaping out into the unknown
      Letting go of familiar worlds
        And slipping into a field of surrender
          Where only the courageous are invited

The air is unruffled and silky
  That guides his effortless freefall
    Invisible wings take over his downward flight
      There is nothing to do
        But embrace the wonder
          The fullness of it all
            Accepting the inevitable trajectory
          Into the arms of what is
          And what will be

His sculpted body pierces a portal
  Through the water's crust
    Plunges deep within the ocean depths
      Disappears into the blue vastness
        The droplets which caress his body
          Were born from the one ocean
            That crash gentle waves
          Upon every distant shore

He is immersed within the womb
  Of this ubiquitous world
    Where timeless sea creatures
      Chant their ancient songs
        Heard by the divers
          Who daringly seek
            To be reborn by their hallowed music
              To embody their sublime pageantry
          And to dance
            In their revelations of freedom

For a never-ending instant
   The music engulfs him
      Consumes him - transforms him
         He effortlessly merges
            With the symphonic matrix of the oceanic
               The canticle of the deep
                  To become the singer
                     The singing - and the song

Ultimately the primal urgency for air
   To fill his lungs with breath
      Magnetizes him toward the surface
         To the next edge of infinity
            Where he yearns to offer his virtuosity
               To an ever blossoming world

He emerges from the blue water
   Placing his feet upon a fragile Earth
      Knowing that to dive into freedom
         Is to rediscover
            The immeasurable treasures of the gods

For now everything has suddenly changed
   His eager eyes again gaze out in all directions
      Yet he simply notices
         That even though the totality of the Universe
            Has mysteriously awakened
               There is still another precipice to explore
                  On the next horizon

# Introduction to the Poem - _A Taste Of Perfection_

THIS POEM ORIGINATED FROM SPIRITED DIALOGUES with my camping partner as the sun was rising over distant pine trees in the early morning air. Because of his empowering philosophy of life, my introspective friend would frequently proclaim the phrase, "Life Is perfect" - and would clarify what he meant by sharing his belief that God created a perfect world.

Of course, conversely, there are scores of people who think the world is anything but perfect. There is so much abject suffering in the lives of a large measure of humanity from their diverse experiences of hardships and misfortunes. How could life be perfect when disturbing adversity or intense pain is happening in one's life?

The life we each experience daily is full of paradox. This poem was written to help address the existential paradox of _absolute perfection_ versus _personal evolution_. Could our life be unfolding perfectly just the way it is - and, simultaneously, could it be the mission of every one of us to do our best to help make the world a little more perfect?

✳    ✳    ✳    ✳

# Circle of Existential Paradoxes
## (In Relation to the Transcendent and Material Realms of Life)

**BEING /**
**BECOMING**

*TRANSCENDENT:*
MY LIFE IS UNFOLDING
PERFECTLY JUST AS IT IS
*+SIMULTANEOUSLY+*
*MATERIAL:*
ALL OF LIFE IS EVOLVING
TO HELP THE WORLD
BECOME MORE PERFECT

**ETERNITY /**
**TIME**

*TRANSCENDENT:*
LIFE IS ETERNAL
*+SIMULTANEOUSLY+*
*MATERIAL:*
ALL FORMS OF LIFE
LIVE IN A PHYSICAL
BODY THAT ONE DAY
WILL END IN TIME

**ONENESS /**
**DUALITY**

*TRANSCENDENT:*
ALL OF CREATION
IS ONE UNITY
*+SIMULTANEOUSLY+*
*MATERIAL:*
LIFE IS EXPERIENCE
IN A BODY OF MANY
DIVERSE POLARITIES

**PURE CONSCIOUSNESS /**
**CREATION**

*TRANSCENDENT:*
*PURE CONSCIOUSNESS* (OR
*THE SOURCE*) IS THE CAUSE
OF ALL LIFE EXPERIENCE
*+SIMULTANEOUSLY+*
*MATERIAL:*
MATERIAL EXPRESSION IS
*CONSCIOUSNESS* IN FORM

# A Taste Of Perfection

Who has the audacity to proclaim they are perfect?
What breed of person would brazenly stand up
To fabricate this boisterous declaration?
Yet could there possibly be some veracity here
Some brand of original zest
Some novel flavor of perfection
For us to sample at life's lavish banquet table?

We all recognize a shadowy flavor of possibility
Spiced with the petty sin of arrogance
Of burying one's head in the thick sands of denial
Not able to divulge the unavoidable childhood scars
Or the vast array of personality flaws
Wounds disturbing the neat and tidy weavings
Within the hollow fabric of one's living

Of course there's an alternate taste - seasoned with a salty awareness
Which from the lofty supernal vista of an eagle
Looking down upon the chronicle of our lives
Decrees that all of life
In some incomprehensible manner - is unfolding perfectly
And from this omniscient vantage
It's the only game in town

From this exalted and sanctified view
Where the entire enterprise can be witnessed as it is
My life can only be perfect
Which naturally arises from the terrestrial radiance of the Earth
Which is perfect just the way it is
Which arises from the stellar radiance of the Solar System
Which is perfect the way it is
Which arises from the galactic radiance of the Milky Way
Which of course is also perfect

As the entire Universe is perfect
　　And as everything within all of Creation
　　　　Is perfectly perfect

Yet how could this be?
　　How could my life really be perfect?
　　　　I have constant problems
　　　　　　Disturbances - challenges
　　　　　　　　I experience frequent torments
　　　　　　　　　　Of pain and anguish
　　　　　　　　　　　　I stub my toe
　　　　　　　　　　　　　　I argue with my Beloved
　　　　　　　　　　　　　　　　I am afraid to be my true self
　　　　　　　　　　　　　　　　　　The list goes on and on

Wait a minute - let me stray back
　　To summon up what my purpose truly is
　　　　For the undertaking of a lifetime ride
　　　　　　On this blue orb of a planet
　　　　　　　　Through titanic darkness of empty space

From my roller coaster ride thus far
　　The impression I get is that purpose is about learning
　　　　To fully love all of life in every moment
　　　　　　And to have the most enchanting time along the way

So from my bird's-eye view
　　These disturbances
　　　　Seem to be the necessary food
　　　　　　Laid out for me on life's banquet table
　　　　　　　　The gifts and blessings provided
　　　　　　　　　　To nourish my heart ever further
　　　　　　　　　　　　So a new stream of *Love's* embrace
　　　　　　　　　　　　　　Can wrap its arms around me
　　　　　　　　　　　　　　　　Helping me fulfill my destiny
　　　　　　　　　　　　　　　　　　And ultimately do
　　　　　　　　　　　　　　　　　　　　What I have faithfully come here to do

If stubbing my toe
    Arguing with my Beloved
        Or being afraid to be myself is really a gift
            So I can dive deeper
                Into the sacred ocean of *Immeasurable Love*
                    And accept myself - and all of life - just as it is
                        While letting go of attachments
                            To my misguided agenda
                                Then could it be that every event
                                    Is a deified blessing from the banquet table
                                        Flavored with the taste
                                            Of constant development
                                                Of continual expansion
                                                    Of perpetual awakening
                                                        To my next unfathomable sphere
                                                            Of glorious emergence?

Yes - that sounds like perfection
    The natural advancement of infinite blossoming
        The luminous majesty of unfurling existence
            Opening in a way which can only be perfect
                Because every facet of life
                    Is simply unfolding the way it is
                        And if the lives of amoebas - and mosquitoes - and aardvarks
                            As well as my own life - are simply the way they are
                                Then my journey through it
                                    Must be unfolding perfectly

By God - I have just uncovered
    The audacity to declare
        And stand here before you
            With my *Soul's* ferociousness
                To shout into the heavens
                    That yes - my life is perfect

And - Ouch!!! - Damn it!!!
    I just stubbed my toe again

✳

✳  ·  ✳

✳

# Introduction to the Poem – _You Are A Diamond_

IT HAS BEEN SAID BY ARTISTS AND POETS that we are each "a diamond in the rough". _Life's_ constant invitation is for us to love and accept ourselves completely and unconditionally while embracing all of our "rough" individual flaws and personality traits. This lifelong invitation includes a heightened recognition that the challenging parts of our life do not have to be seen as problems - but can be construed as sacred gifts that we use to "polish the diamond" within us.

We can use these occasions or "gifts from life" to elevate our consciousness so we may transform into a more radiant expression of our highest self. Thus, we attain a more expanded awareness - not by being habitually attached to getting rid of our suffering or challenges - but through the daily surrender of embracing each challenge as "a gift in disguise" that we can utilize for our personal and collective transformation. These are life's exquisite opportunities to let our pain or challenging experiences point us to what really matters - and what our life is truly about.

Every one of us is a living masterpiece that's endlessly evolving - a creative work in progress. Our life is the outer creative expression of our inner development. We are continually learning to courageously unveil the exquisite beauty and majesty of who we truly are.

This poem was written as a declaration that each day we artistically fashion the blank canvas of our life to reveal the next version of our masterpiece.

❊   ❊   ❊   ❊

This poem is included in each of the four volumes of **Journey of _The Great Circle_** by Oman Ken – a book series of daily transformative practices.

# Circle of the Quest for Inner Freedom
## (The Natural Yearning to Live an Awakened Life)

**TRUE NATURE**
**(FORMLESS TRANSCENDENT)**
*"THE ONE"*
MY *TRUE NATURE* IS ABOUT:
+ ALIGNING WITH
*THE SOURCE OF LIFE*
+ BEING FULLY PRESENT
+ REALIZING THAT WHO
I REALLY AM IS ETERNAL
+ EMBRACING PERFECTION

**PURPOSE**
(INTERIOR YEARNING)
EVOLUTION OF
MY CONSCIOUSNESS
MY PURPOSE IS ABOUT:
+ LEARNING
+ EXPANDING
+ DEVELOPING
+ AWAKENING

**MISSION**
(EXTERIOR YEARNING)
EVOLUTION OF
MY CREATIVITY
MY MISSION IS ABOUT:
+ CREATING
+ EXPRESSING
+ TRANSFORMING
+ CONTRIBUTING

**MEANING**
(RELATED TO FORM)
*"THE MANY"*
THE MEANING OF MY LIFE IS
ABOUT:
+ SERVING
+ LOVING
+ GIVING
+ OFFERING KINDNESS

# You Are A Diamond

You are a perfect diamond
   Longing to become more perfect
     A luminescent jewel
       Shimmering upon the necklace
         Of this ephemeral world
           Forged from the supreme fire
             Within the heart of the Universe

You are a multifaceted gem
   Of sublime majesty and grace
     Through which *Life* focuses its celestial starlight
     So it may glisten endlessly within you

You are a beloved *artist of life*
   Fashioning unparalleled hues
     Upon the blank canvas of each new day
       To create the next rendering
         Of your magnificent masterpiece

You are an invincible prism of the *Soul*
   Chiseled into form
     So *the Fullness* of the Cosmos can savor
       More of the luminous spectrum
         Of its sensual wonders and hallowed glories

You are an ascending aeronaut spiraling heavenwards
   Climbing the infinite ladder of possibility
     Navigating tumultuous storms and immaculate skies
     Terrestrial chaos and galactic order
       The sacred gifts you use
         To share the omniscient nature
           Of your truest self

You are a sovereign sculptor of untethered intentions
Each one polishing the ever-effulgent diamond of your life
So you may launch new portals of pristine freedom
For the invisible lines of destiny
To dance through you

Your mission - to dance with the *Light*
Your purpose - to polish the perfection
Your meaning of it all - to give for the good of all

It's just what diamonds
Who spend their life *Being*
In the course of *Becoming*
Do

# Introduction to the Poem – _The Wheel Of Seasons_

THIS POEM WAS WRITTEN to explore "the Big Picture Perspective of Life" - or what some contemporary philosophers have referred to as "the perspective of life that is portrayed within _The Great Circle_". _The Great Circle_ is a four-quadrant map illustrating the interior and exterior aspects of life. For example: consciousness and creation - Spirit and body - inward expansion and outward expression.

I define _The Great Circle_, from a spiritual point-of-view, as "a spiritual map of an awakening life". The four quadrants of _The Great Circle_ illustrate four universal dynamics that describe the evolutionary unfolding of every phenomenon within the Universe and the natural world - as well as the primary dynamics within each of our lives.

One of the essential dynamics of _The Great Circle_ is that life includes a Transcendent Reality of Oneness - an Absolute Unity of All That Is. Our conscious awareness of this dynamic can help us experience that everything in our lives, and every facet of the Earth and Universe, is deeply interconnected as one universal energy.

The poem also investigates the following statement of possibility:

"What a sacred gift it would be for all of humanity,
and for the entire Earth,
if we each knew we were intimately connected
together as one global family
- a grand blessing for all people
and for every form of life."

✳    ✳    ✳    ✳

# The Great Circle
## (A Spiritual Map of an Awakening Life)

**"THE ONE"**
PERFECT ONENESS,
UNITY WITHOUT FORM,
THE ONE TRANSCENDENT
SOURCE OF ALL THAT IS,
INFINITE INTELLIGENCE,
LIMITLESS LOVE,
MY *TRUE NATURE*
WHICH IS ETERNAL
*(BEING)*

**INNER DEVELOPMENT**
INWARD EXPANSION
OF MY AWARENESS
+
INTERIOR EVOLVING
CONSCIOUSNESS
+
MY SPIRITUAL
AWAKENING
*(BECOMING)*

**OUTER TRANSFORMATION**
OUTWARD EXPRESSION
OF MY HEALING
+
EXTERIOR EVOLVING
CREATIVITY
+
MY CONSCIOUS
CONTRIBUTION
*(BECOMING)*

**"THE MANY"**
THE PERFECTION WITHIN
EACH FORM OF LIFE,
THE MANY UNIQUE
FORMS WITHIN NATURE,
INCLUDING MY BODY, ALL
UNFOLDING PERFECTLY
IN THE PRESENT MOMENT
*(BEING)*

49

# The Wheel Of Seasons

As an eager euphoric young boy
  I meandered my way
    Into a mammoth cathedral-like chamber
      Fashioned with high thick glass windows
        Between me and a menagerie of sea creatures
          Darting about inside a blue-green empire
            Harbored within a nearby ocean aquarium

Every diverse sliver of earthen life
  Has triumphantly emerged from primordial seas
    Dandelions - salamanders - porcupines
      Octopuses - hippopotami - and a billion other species
        All birthed - not only from the ancestry of prodigious oceans
          But from the omniscient Womb of Creation itself

Like the arduous journey of climbing down
  A long seemingly endless stairway
    Within a tall multi-tiered building
      Passing slowly from floor to lower floor
        Life ingeniously descended
          The long fractal trek of countless expressions
            From galaxy to star system - from planet to amoeba
              From reptile to mammal
                Finally landing at base level
                  The hallowed ground
                    Where I now stand stoutly on two legs

In the fullness of time two-leggeds learned
  About the other kinsfolk from their water-laden planet
    The innumerable sea creatures
      And immeasurable terrestrial progeny
        All revolving in a uniform orbit
          Around a stellar inferno

Then - so as to communicate
  This glorious revelation to neighboring tribes
    Some devised their mythical story - a Great Story of Awakening
      A universal journey of human life infinitely advancing
        Placing four seasonal designations
          Upon the cardinal phases of a tribe's progression
            Within the globe's recurring rotation into ever greater glory
            Marking Summer into Autumn - Winter into Spring
            The terrestrial saga of one unfolding revolution
          Around a fiery star

The Great Story of orbital rhythms
  Is rooted in the cyclical chapter of Winter
    Silent - eternal - limitless - *"The One"*
      Like a towering mountain keeping still
        Yet with Winter's ear always attentive to
          Life's perpetual song of yearning - of awakening
        With an inborn mandate to mirror its melodies
          And transform them into a symphonic masterpiece

A partial rotation to the next chapter
  Heralds the exultant festival of Spring
    Where the promise of another flowering is expressed
      Metamorphosing into an iconic tree of creativity
        Branching outward into the arms of contribution
        Transforming into myriad patterns of hope
      From the eminent commands
        Given by an *Inner Captain*
          Who rules Winter's majestic schooner

The further turning of the Wheel
  Dives into the iconic ocean of Summer
    The chapter pointing to a self-organizing universe
      Built within the immortal walls
        Of generosity and a kind heart
        The collective home of *"The Many"*
          A plethora of nature's gardens in abundance

As the Wheel spins into Autumn
   A burning impulse rouses an essential yearning to awaken
      To reach toward a higher edge - an uncharted horizon
        To view new untethered worlds
          With the panoramic eyes of an eagle
            Soaring above verdant landscapes
              Developing generous perspectives
                And learning superior possibilities

We address divergent seasonal chapters
   As four singular spokes of the Wheel
      Yet from the cradle of absolute wholeness
        It's simply one revolution
          Around a small but magnificent star

We build stories around multiple phases of the moon
   Yet from the crucible of unity
      It's simply one revolution
        Of a small orbiting celestial body

And we speak about the isolated monuments of existence
   Galaxies - stars - rocks - vegetation - four-leggeds - you and me
      Yet from a humble place where we may not yet understand
        It's simply one animated tapestry
          A dance of countless waves within a solitary Ocean
            A radiant sea of interwoven energy in constant motion
              A dimensionless soup of photons and information
                Designed by an *Eternal Cosmic Choreographer*

All *Cosmic Designers* are thoroughly taught
   *How* to utilize "alchemical chambers of quantum creation"
      They employ the ubiquitous laws of physics
        Of geology and biology - of fractal geometry
          From which - inside the chamber
            Mystery fashions into form
              Whatever you passionately intend
            As your heart's desire

On one side of the "miraculous chamber"
   You place an ardent song of intent - a burning impulse of potential
      The next promising edge of your horizon
         The panoramic pledge of your eagle's sight
            Your unexpressed future possibility

On the other side arrives an artfully sculpted masterpiece
   Mirroring the canticle of your most fervent yearning
      A creative manifestation adding to the ascending Tree of Life
         Which grows within a copious garden
            From the benign out-pouring of a *Designer's* sculpting hand

One day we might lucidly determine
   At the core of any "chamber of quantum creation"
      Reigns not only the dazzling enigma
         Of *the Eternal Ocean* and *the Mystery of Life* itself
            But of our own mastery of co-creation

And as I stood mesmerized in awe
   In front of the glass window of that behemoth aquarium
      In the younger years of my living
         A soundless voice whispered to me
            "Who and what you are emerged from this vast Ocean"

Yet simultaneously within a bewildering matrix of existence
   I also heard "You *are* the Ocean"

So I asked myself "Wait a minute - could this be?"
   "I am the Ocean?" - "I am the Universe?"
      "I am That - and That - and That - and even That?"

Since my visit to the aquarium long ago
   I've spent my whole life standing on the edge of a precipice
      The gentle tug of the wind against my body
         Urging me to take the leap
            To constantly inquire into the question
               "What if this were true?"

# Introduction to the Poem – _Leap Of Surrender_

IMAGINE THAT YOU HAVE JUST LEAPED OFF A HIGH CLIFF and there is a deep pool of water below. The moment your feet left the ground you would, most likely, have felt a vigorous sensation of letting go - surrendering to the obvious fact that you're now falling through the air. This flash of surrender is the inner acknowledgement that, for an instant, you've let go of your personal control - and thus, have now yielded control to the natural flow of life - and where this flow is effortlessly taking you. At a heightened spiritual awareness, this would be an experience of fully surrendering to "what is" - what is undeniably true in the present moment.

This poem explores the idea that a "Big Picture vantage" of surrender is like a "Big Picture vantage" of forgiveness. Radical forgiveness requires letting go of our expectations and attachments of how we want life to be - and completely accepting how life actually is. This kind of acceptance leads to the mastery of awakened awareness.

Awakened forgiveness and surrender are cultivated by embracing ever larger and more inclusive perspectives of life. These expansive points-of-view support us in learning and accepting that our life is unfolding perfectly just as it is. This awareness is what the great spiritual teachers and sages have learned to advance - so as to consciously navigate life with mastery.

This poem was written as if the reader is, metaphorically, leaping off "an extremely high precipice of time". As you are reading the poem, imagine that, in the beginning of your descent, you initially are falling through an ancient period of time - eons ago. And as the journey's dive continues through the evolution of the ages, time advances - and moves closer and closer to the present moment.

※　　※　　※　　※

# Circle of Surrender

**LETTING GO**
*SURRENDER* –
MY ABILITY TO LET GO
OF MY ATTACHMENTS
REGARDING HOW I
THINK MY LIFE SHOULD
BE, AND INSTEAD,
EMBRACE WHAT IS

**TRUST**
*SURRENDER* –
MY ABILITY TO TRUST
EVERYTHING IN MY LIFE
TO *A GREATER POWER,*
AND TO THE BENEVO-
LENT UNFOLDING
OF THE UNKNOWN

**RELINQUISHMENT**
*SURRENDER* –
MY ABILITY
TO RELINQUISH
MY HABITUAL NEED TO
CONTROL AND EXPERI-
ENCE THE NATURAL
UNFOLDING OF LIFE

**FLOW**
*SURRENDER* –
MY ABILITY TO BE
FLEXIBLE AND FLOW
WITH THE CONSTANT
CHANGES IN MY LIFE
AS WELL AS WITH
WHATEVER ARISES

# Leap Of Surrender

With a commanding thrust
   I leap off a towering precipice of time
      As I begin my tumultuous descent
         Through layers of sequential ages
            My slackened body submits to a chronicled plunge
               Viewing former lives through the thick air of history

For a horrifying moment
   I am ravaged from the dread of being eaten alive
      Devoured by the instincts of a hungry lion
         Roaming the African savanna with intrepid sovereignty

Today in this lifetime
   Could I fathom this agonizing distress from another vantage
      From the clever words of Lao Tzu
         Who inspires me with his cunning poetry
            Inviting me to audaciously accept the ceaseless current
         Of luminous perfection forever unfolding
            In life's continuum of eternity?

I continue plummeting through the air
   Getting nearer to the unyielding ground
      I gasp in terror as I succumb
         To the deranged brutality of a horrid Inquisition
        As I am barbarously set ablaze
         For the potent vigor of my unwavering beliefs

In today's judicious world
   Could I interpret this hideous affair with insight
      Sensed from the superior words of Lord Krishna
        Conferring with Arjuna on the battlefield
         Declarations tenderly reminding me
            To accept the measures of life as they are
               To relinquish all judgment in the manner it unfolds
            And to vanquish any resistance to what is?

I then descend further still
   Plunging ever closer to the earth below

I meet the crazed insanity of the Holocaust
   The demented act of genocide
      As I am cruelly annihilated
         For the ruthless crime of belonging to my tribe

From where I perceive things now
   Could I reframe this saga with the astute claims of Buddha
      Encouraging me to view the suffering in my world
         From a much different more inclusive stance
            An outlook that is renovated
               By Buddha's massive perspective
                  Of what life is truly about - and what really matters?

I continue to descend further
   Approaching solid ground
      I am urged to let go of the fear of not being enough
         Of being consumed by the hungry opinions of others
         Of being burned by the deranged need to control
         Of being annihilated by my terror of the unknown

This offer carries me to an exalted inhalation
   Living at the core of every breath
      Where I am summoned to perceive all things anew
         Pointing me to the gospels of Jesus
            On the eminent Mount of Olives
               When he prudently spoke of lilies in the field
                  Being cared for without worry or concern for need
               And so with unabridged detachment
               I exhale another breath

Somehow my venturesome fall comes to a close
   By absolutely surrendering to the moment
      Or at long last hitting the Ground - of Being - or maybe both
         Instantly awakening to eternity's illusive dream

Immersed in freedom's whisper
I stand up again - knowing without doubt
I am here to climb once more the ascending stairway
Of another dream - conscious and compassionate
Eager to wholly surrender into the revolutionary flight
Of the next leap

# Introduction to the Poem - _A Wizard of Words_

THIS POEM WAS WRITTEN to symbolize the _epic evolutionary journey of global awakening_ that's taking place right now on our planet within the hearts and minds of every individual.

The simple mythic story told within the poem depicts a collective _journey of discovery, a journey of self-mastery_ that every person upon the Earth is embarked on (whether he or she is consciously aware of it or not). This universal archetypal story is symbolically illustrated in the Contemplation Circle called - the Archetypes of Spiritual Awakening.

The menacing fire dragon represents the dysfunctional self-oriented nature within every individual that must eventually be healed and transformed. The young awakening goddess symbolizes the inner growth unfolding within each person who is dedicated to cultivating personal development and inner freedom. This awakening process is displayed in the Contemplation Circle as the healing and transformation of the archetype of the **Young Awakening Self,** which through time and much life experience, eventually evolves into the **Compassionate Heart**.

The goddess (feminine nature) within us all is overtaken for a time by the dark power of the dragon (the unloving and dysfunctional self that's unconscious within every person), but then, through conscious dedication and inner revelation, is transformed and awakened. _"The One"_ god who abides on the throne of stars represents the archetype of **Infinite Presence**, in other words - **_the Transcendent Nature of Life_**.

When these two aspects of our inner being are merged as one (the joining together of the **Compassionate Heart** with the **Transcendent,** the union of the "Servant of Love" with the "_Mind of God_"), then this sublime merging is the ultimate realization of the Fully Awakened Self, the **Master of Freedom,** that is destined to be embodied and fully lived within each one of us.

✳   ✳   ✳   ✳

This poem is included in the **Spring Volume** of **Journey of _The Great Circle_** by Oman Ken - a book of daily transformative practices.

# Circle of Archetypes of Spiritual Awakening
## (My Spiritual Journey of Personal Transformation)

**MASTER OF FREEDOM**
MY AWARENESS AS I LIVE
AN AWAKENED LIFE
OF INNER FREEDOM - AND
LOVE UNCONDITIONALLY
+ MY COMPASSIONATE
HEART FULLY MERGED
WITH *INFINITE PRESENCE*

**YOUNG AWAKENING SELF**
THIS IS MY LEVEL
OF AWARENESS WHEN
I AM SELF-CENTERED,
FOCUSED ON APPROVAL,
ATTACHMENT, CONTROL,
SELF-POWER, OR FEAR,
YET YEARN TO AWAKEN

*INFINITE PRESENCE*
*"THE ONE", THE SOURCE*
*OF LIFE, UNIVERSAL*
*CONSCIOUSNESS, GOD,*
*INFINITE INTELLIGENCE,*
*LIMITLESS LOVE, THE*
*TRANSCENDENT SELF,*
*MY ETERNAL NATURE*

**COMPASSIONATE HEART**
MY LEVEL OF AWARENESS
AS I CONSCIOUSLY LIVE
A WORLD-CENTERED LIFE
THAT IS COMPASSIONATE,
CARING, GRATEFUL
FOR LIFE, AND IN SERVICE
TO THE GOOD OF ALL

# A Wizard Of Words

They all marched through the night to a rattle of crickets
    Half asleep as if ambling in a dream
        Lumbering through the dark pine forest
            Their throbbing hearts longing to be awake

From the four winds - they were each drawn in
    Like hypnotized moths magnetized to flame
        Captured by a spellbound gravity
            Seized by a circle of mesmerizing radiance
                Until all stood waiting in the open clearing
                    Where a raging bonfire blazed
                        Reaching for the canopy of starlight

Dancing flames dashed wide illuminating the superior form of a man
    As he poured his gaze into each heart
        While pacing around the warm glowing circle
        Among this eager assemblage of listeners

He was a wizard of words
    A magician of spoken language with a timeless story on his tongue
        Arranging tonal images in perfect sequence
            Like polychrome beaded necklaces artfully crafted
                Or patterned rows of flowers within a regal garden
            Stretching their vivid petals toward the sun

Each mind was locked on his words
    As an epic saga began to unfurl
        An iconic tale of a menacing dragon breathing fire
        Living its sordid days near the kingdom
            Terrorizing those who dwelt upon this fragile world
            With malicious chains of suffering
            The shackles of ruthless control
                Coercing the air into a dungeon of fear and death

Then - over the turns of time the dragon applied its cleverness
　　To capture the greatest jewel within the kingdom
　　　　The young awakening goddess
　　　　　　Whose very essence inhabited the heart of every village dweller

The goddess was overtaken - intoxicated by the dragon's elixir of dark magic
　　Entranced by its glamorous illusions
　　　　Dazed into submission by its hypnotic induction
　　　　　　Yet at the same time she could hear the chant of an incessant voice
　　　　　　　　Intoning *an intimate love song* that beckoned from somewhere within

The dragon's manacles held the goddess captive
　　Hopelessly imprisoned in her solitary tower
　　　　Chained to an ancient wall of ignorance
　　　　　　Bound by blind self-delusion
　　　　　　　　Wings clipped and broken - unable to soar

Yet all the while *"The One"* who is eternal and benevolent
　　Who everlastingly abides on the throne of stars
　　　　Who perpetually invokes the natural longings within every god and goddess
　　　　　　Waited patiently for her with his hallowed offerings
　　　　　　　　Invisible - translucent in his dominion of seeming paradoxes
　　　　　　　　　　Witnessing the ceaseless play of light and darkness
　　　　　　　　　　　　The unfolding spiral of body and *Soul*
　　　　　　　　　　　　　　Within *"The Many"* forms of the world
　　　　　　　　　　　　　　The constant wheel of seasons

The storyteller's words became the pages of the night
　　Like a book illustrating life's visions of tomorrow's potential
　　　　Displaying celestial possibilities for all children of the kingdom
　　　　　　And awakening the passion for liberty
　　　　　　　　In each listener's heart

The wizard's words chronicled a turning point - revolving around her inner revelation
　　A profound epiphany - a leap of awareness that transformed everything
　　　　As she unreservedly embraced the transcendent offerings of *"The One"*
　　　　　　And unrestrainedly dove into his *Ocean* amid the throne of stars

Through reams of quaking inquiry from her questioning heart
The goddess cultivated waves of surrender - a blanket of acceptance
And gratitude wildly rippling within her core
Which all gently merged into a sea of Oneness
Until she and *the Translucent One* were utterly fused
As droplets from his *Ocean* baptized her crown
Unfurled her wings - she began to free herself
Shaking the entire Universe into a new pattern of possibility

And now a once sleeping goddess
Who had awakened a soaring desire within her *Soul*
Through her communion of becoming one with his *Eternal Gift*
Miraculously dispatched her prayer
Carried by a messenger angel
On a brazen arrow flung by her supple bow
Perfectly arriving at its destined target
Burying itself deep into the bones of the dragon
Until its terrorizing fire and fear
Were extinguished

All of its dragonfire melted into a hallowed song
For without its deceptive mask and trickery
The dragon was truly seen
Beyond its scales of illusion
To be the gift of *Light*
At the center of every living form
And was revealed to be an immortal friend
That was forever alert within the kingdom
Warding off any future threat of foe or malice

The holy song revealed a new heaven and a new earth
In such a way that god and goddess were intimately joined
Ageless lovers in blissful communion
A miracle of transmutation
Metamorphosis of two now one
Birthing a mastery of life
That constantly bowed to Mystery

All could hear the exalted hymn
   Of two beloveds entwined in the arms of compassion
      Like the mother ocean that's always caressing
         Each of her untethered river children

Of twin winged lovers merged in sacred union
   Birthed within the womb of creation
      From which all star clusters and planets
         Offer their simple melodies
            In some synchronized cosmic symphony

Then - for a lingering moment
   The impresario of words was still
      Like a blue heron
         Anchored next to a forest stream
            Allowing for an ever deeper story
               To display its heart-wisdom within the burning silence

They all closed their eyes
   As he stood firm and motionless for a very long time
      Two legs balanced
         Body and *Soul* aligned
            Both supporting his paradoxical Universe
               *The Silent Witness* on one side
                  The Servant of *Love* on the other

When their eyes opened - he was gone
   So one by one
      The band of listeners re-entered the dawning light of the woods
         Carrying their new treasure with them
            As if it were precious gold upon their shoulders
               Returning to their warm firesides
                  In homes of far-off villages
                     Eager to bestow the sacred gift they received
                        To share the story from the wizard of words
                     With all of their children

# III

# STAIRWAYS TO EVOLUTIONARY SPIRITUALITY

# Introduction to the Poem - _The Hologram_

A PHOTOGRAPHIC HOLOGRAM IS A DEVICE which is constructed in such a manner that if you project a coherent light onto the hologram's photographic plate, it will display a 3D like image. If you break the initial hologram into two or more pieces - and shine a light on one of the pieces, it will display the complete image. In other words, if a light is projected onto any individual piece of the hologram, which was separated from the full photographic plate, it will still display the entire original image.

Thus, the hologram is a good metaphor for illustrating how we can examine components of reality at smaller and smaller scales - such as cells, molecules, atoms, and sub-atomic particles. Whenever you observe any part of the natural world, the same _Infinite Intelligence_ - the same _Universal Life Energy_ - the same _God-Force_ - is always present. No matter how we divide "the stuff of life" into little pieces and specific categories, there remains the same Oneness - the same Absolute Unity - the same Transcendent Presence - existing within all things.

This poem was written to explore how the poetic "heart language" of religion - and the "evidence-based language" of science - can both point us to the realization that there is a Majesty of Oneness within all of life.

# Circle of *Being* and *Becoming*
## (A Paradox of Simultaneous and Complimentary Realms of My Life)

*PERFECTION* –
### PATH OF EVOLUTION
*BEING* - THE REALIZATION,
IN THIS MOMENT, MY LIFE
IS UNFOLDING PERFECTLY
*+SIMULTANEOUSLY+*
*BECOMING* - MY *JOURNEY
OF DISCOVERY* TO HELP
THE WORLD EVOLVE AND
BECOME MORE PERFECT

*PRESENCE* –
### PATH OF TIME
*BEING* - EXPERIENCING
MY LIFE FULLY IN THE
PRESENT MOMENT
*+SIMULTANEOUSLY+*
*BECOMING* - MY INNER
*SPIRITUAL JOURNEY*
IN WHICH I CREATE
A BETTER FUTURE

*LIMITLESS LOVE* –
### PATH OF MY LIFE
*BEING* - EXPERIENCING
EVERY MOMENT AS
*LIMITLESS LOVE*
*+SIMULTANEOUSLY+*
*BECOMING* – MY *JOURNEY
TO LOVE*, WHICH IS "ALL
WITHIN MY LIFE THAT
NEEDS DEVELOPMENT"

*ETERNAL SELF* –
### PATH OF EXPERIENCE
*BEING* - MY *ETERNAL SELF,
PURE CONSCIOUSNESS,*
WHICH IS UNBOUNDED
*+SIMULTANEOUSLY+*
*BECOMING* - THE JOURNEY
OF MY LIFE EXPERIENCE
AWAKENING ME TO A LIFE
OF INNER FREEDOM

# Hologram

I wish I could have been there
  When you audaciously declared to all of us
    Through the voice of your messianic prophet
      Standing on a sun-drenched rocky hillside
        Amidst the feeding multitudes
          That "I and the Father are one"

Yet I'm grateful to be here now
  As you boldly herald once again
    With a brand new arrangement of words
      Through the voices of your messianic physicists
        Who daringly stand at spotlight-drenched podiums
          In multitudes of universities and science institutions
            Proclaiming "Everything in the Universe
              Emerged from *an Unbounded Ocean and Unified Field*
            *The One Source* and 'Cosmic Father'
           *Of all that has been created"*

Two thousand years ago
  We all ached for a soothing heart language
    As your nurturing words melted gracefully
      Into the cradle of our timely needs

Today we are being kissed and wooed
  By a lover's language of your science-based knowledge
    Pages of the Holy Scriptures of Evolution
      Telling your Great Story of Awakening
        Of a Universe exploding with creativity
          Sculpting multifarious diversity
            Infinitely blossoming like a lotus flower

Religion - serving the flowering of the heart
  The hallowed embrace of *Being*

Science - serving the flowering of the mind
  The perpetual partaking of *Becoming*

*Becoming* is like boldly walking out on a high precipice
  Heroically diving into the bourgeoning hologram
    Of your flawless Universe
      Meandering through its 13.8 billion year odyssey
        Embarking on its endless arrow
          Of development and creative wizardry

*Being* is like gently pounding on the Universe
  With a soft delicate hammer of life-affirming questions
    Then breaking off a small piece of your vast hologram
      So I can shine through it
        The *Light* of my *True Essential Nature*
          In order to behold within me
            The Fullness and Unity of existence

From this unfathomable Oneness came
  The initial primal explosion of luminance
    Then the torrential sculpting of unfurling galaxies and stars
      And the supernova furnaces
        That fashioned stardust into solar systems
          So myriad life forms on a billion planets could find their origin

So I could swim in the sundry oceans of religion
  And awake to the emergent revelations of science
    Of *Being* and *Becoming*
      The continuum of *Light* which illuminates my hologram
        From the clouds of illusion
          That I may dance wildly and naked
            In *a Field of Shimmering Love*

Knowing that I am a tiny sliver
  Of your gargantuan Cosmic Hologram
    Does that make me a god too
      Or a chip off the old block?

# Introduction to the Poem – _Infinite Awakenings_

THIS STORY POEM WAS INSPIRED by the first few pages of the book, "The New Earth" by the spiritual teacher Eckhart Tolle - and by a powerful personal transformative experience of epiphany.

It was written in the spring of 2008 when I traveled to Brazil with an open heart and an intention to experience a physical healing from the Brazilian psychic healer, John of God. While at the John of God Healing Center, I had a profound spiritual epiphany of Oneness - and wrote this poem as part of an embodiment of that experience.

In his book Eckhart describes how at one time, millions of years ago, there was a plethora of green vegetation on the planet, yet there were no plants in the form of flowers. The beautiful manifestation of flowers had not yet arrived on the evolutionary scene. But over time and with gradual biological development, _Life_ eventually found a way to empower a brand new emergent form to arise, the very first flower.

For the first flower to take shape on Earth, a radical shift in consciousness was required within the plant kingdom. This new expression of vegetative structure could be thought of as an "enlightenment" or "awakening" of the plant kingdom.

A similar kind of radical shift in consciousness also occurred in the mineral kingdom with the first diamond - and millions of years later, in the animal kingdom with the first flight of a primordial bird.

The same expansive evolutionary impulses in consciousness are happening right now throughout the world as they continuously have from the beginning of the Earth. Each person on the planet is now, consciously or unconsciously, evolving and developing into his or her sacred destiny as an awakened human.

✳   ✳   ✳   ✳

This poem is included in the **Winter Volume** of **Journey of _The Great Circle_** by Oman Ken - a book of daily transformative practices.

# Circle of Infinite Awakenings
## (Progressive Images of Emergent Evolution)

**FIRST AWAKENED HUMAN**
THE TRANSFORMATION OF A FEARFUL SELF-ORIENTED PERSON INTO THE FIRST ENLIGHTENED HUMAN WAS AN *"AWAKENING"* WITHIN HUMANITY

**FIRST DIAMOND**
THE TRANSFORMATION OF CARBON ATOMS INTO THE CRYSTALLINE FORM OF THE FIRST DIAMOND WAS AN *"AWAKENING"* OF THE MINERAL KINGDOM

**FIRST BIRD**
THE TRANSFORMATION OF A LAND REPTILE INTO THE FIRST BIRD THAT TOOK FLIGHT WAS AN *"AWAKENING"* OF THE ANIMAL KINGDOM

**FIRST FLOWER**
THE TRANSFORMATION OF GREEN VEGETATION INTO THE DELICATE FORM OF THE FIRST FLOWER WAS AN *"AWAKENING"* OF THE PLANT KINGDOM

# Infinite Awakenings

A noble princess will display an audacious string of gems
   A jeweled necklace glistening against her bronze skin
      A primal ribbon of ancient geology resting upon her heart
         As precious translucent stones reflect the fiery Sun

Yet a billion revolutions of this solar light - long ago
   Soon after the Earth was fashioned into circular form
      These crystalline jewels did not exist

Until the primordial dancers of minerals and molecules
   Heard the whispers of a new creation song
      And choreographed themselves into fractal ordered lattices
         By the unseen power of some mysterious sculptor's hand
      Awakening the first diamond

Mythic kings and simple peasants alike
   Adorned their regal palaces and pastoral mud huts
      With ornamented gardens of speckled flowers
         That would daily drink the god-like nectar
      Of the falling sunlight

Yet 100 million seasonal cycles - eons ago
   These blossoming creatures of kaleidoscopic color
      Had not yet emerged

Until green leafy pioneers
   Heard the hypnotic allurings of a new unparalleled melody
      And catapulted their way
         Into visions of unexplored frontiers
            Giving birth to a unique pattern of natural artistry
         Awakening the first flower

Poets and traveling troubadours
Throughout the spinning of centuries
Have heralded the hallowed majesty
Of the wondrous flight of birds
That ceaselessly point us inward
To a timeless freedom

These winged magicians of the skies
With their interlaced feathers unfurled
Glide with ease to the edge of starlight

Yet many millions of fleeting winters - so long ago
These heaven bound miracles
Had not yet discovered the secret
To the unfathomable craft of flight

Until heavy scale-covered reptiles
Morphed through time
Into wings of promise
And leaped off cliffs of yesterday
To triumphantly soar with plumed wings
Awakening the first bird

In every silent corner of the world
It's happening once again
Journeyers on a sacred pilgrimage
Like you and me
Saints and sinners
The rich and poor
Awakening to a natural instinctual call

Yet thousands of capricious lifetimes ago
These simple mystic journeyers
Had not yet arrived

Until brave visionary warriors
   Krishna - Buddha - Lao Tzu - Jesus
     And multitudes of the nameless ones
       Held high the sword of truth
        Poked their *Souls*
          Through the one great portal
           Would not take their eyes away
           From the sublime *Light* within
            And merged with the purest field
           Of unbounded stillness
              Becoming the first awakened humans

And the heavens rejoiced
   Each time a new chorus from creation's canticle was sung

As the first precious diamond awakened
   For every princess to adorn her neck

     As the first radiant flower awakened
       Adding celestial majesty to each of our gardens

       As the first soaring bird awakened
         That we might dream of our own flight one day

         As the first human awakened
          Inviting us all to sing a verse of the One Song

I wonder – how some glorious future species
   Gazing up at the star strung sky
     And asking brazen questions
       Will fully embrace the infinite possibilities
        Of the ever-unfolding frequencies of light
      In the next awakening

## Introduction to the Poem - _Emergence_

IN THE SUMMER OF 2017, I enjoyed a camping trip at a site I call "Paradise" in the high country of Arizona. During one brisk morning as the rising sun was very low on the horizon, I was contemplating the word _emergence_. Emergence, from a scientific perspective, is a phenomenon in evolution in which a species, such as a certain bird or frog, will suddenly manifest a whole new set of qualities, due to a long period of evolutionary adaptation to environmental conditions.

During my contemplation, I began to explore how a sudden leap in my current state of consciousness (a profound and rapid expansion of my inner awareness) is like a sudden evolutionary leap (or emergence) that has been taking place in millions of diverse species for billions of years within the wilds of Nature.

I realized that an expansion of my consciousness was directly connected to the expansion of my ability to forgive. And that an expansion of my forgiveness was connected to an expansion of my consciousness. Everything is part of one Great Circle.

I also sensed that a sudden leap of consciousness was connected to what some spiritual teachers refer to as "spontaneous healing", or "a miracle", or what I personally call "emergent healing". All these ideas yearned to find a way to be expressed into words - which became the unfolding of this poem.

⁎    ⁎    ⁎    ⁎

# Circle of Emergence

## A SUDDEN APPEARANCE
*EMERGENCE* –
THE SUDDEN APPEARANCE
OF A BRAND NEW
CHARACTERISTIC
OR UNIQUE QUALITY
OF EXPRESSION

## A LEAP IN EVOLUTION
*EMERGENCE* –
AN INEXPLICABLE,
AND SEEMINGLY
MIRACULOUS, QUANTUM
LEAP OF AWARENESS IN
THE ARC OF EVOLUTION

## A LEAP IN CONSCIOUSNESS
*EMERGENCE* –
THE SUDDEN PHYSICAL
OUT-PICTURING
OF A NEW FORM OF LIFE
DUE TO AN INNER LEAP
IN CONSCIOUSNESS

## A NEW PARADIGM
*EMERGENCE* –
THE MYSTERIOUS
MANIFESTATION
OF A NEW PARADIGM
OF POSSIBILITY ARISING
OUT OF ACCUMULATING
EXPERIENCES OVER TIME

# Emergence

Butterflies did not always adorn Nature's gardens
At one distinct moment eons ago
There were no hovering butterflies
Yet astoundingly in the next
The first butterfly came into view
For this marvel to come about
A slithery creature had to shroud itself
In a coffin-like cocoon
Then wriggle into freedom
So it could take wing

A unique scheme of wondrous emergence
Sculpted the physiques of amoebas and dragonflies
Jellyfish and rhinoceros
Dinosaurs and condors
And of course the volatile arrival of Homo sapiens

At one morning's dawn
During this epic evolutionary exploration
There were no humans
Then suddenly before the millennia's sunset
They were placing their teakettles on stoves
While igniting within their aspiring hearts
The flame of endless possibility

Auspicious fires danced wildly
Tepid liquid began to simmer
With each buoyant choice of evolution's will
The mounting blaze advanced
Within the promising energy of planetary change
Heralding a sanctified pledge
Of clever innovation
Of progressive transmutation

This saga grew to a fevered intensity
    Until substance boiled forth within the global teapot
        So new phases of creation
            Could burst into expression
                The teakettle's whistle exploded into song
                    As ten thousand new species appeared
                        Through a portal of limitless artistry

Then after a billion inventive years
    Of flamboyant original story
        Transmuting into the unparalleled nativities
            Of countless diverse creatures
                There I lay - in my nakedness

I remember the kettle of my life heating up
    When I was early on in years
        My father's leather belt
            Fiercely hammering my backside
                Feeling the wretched pain
                    Of his bewildered strife
                        Enduring the abrasive abuse of authority
                            While erecting a demonic wall of hate
                                Between me and my elusive freedom

Years of striving to dismantle the barricade
    Hellishly attempting to remove the stone
        Which at times seemed too monstrous to lift
            Until one day immersed in a hallowed grace
                I glimpsed my father's radiance within a light reborn
                    I was able to disperse the obscuring fog
                        To forgive the fractured insanity
                            To embrace my illusory demon

Immediately I heard the teakettle's whistle
    Gloriously echo its liberating canticle
        As I added one more helium balloon
            To my multihued collection

I remember the water growing hotter
  The tumultuous day I discovered my wife
    Making love to another
      Being enraged at her infidelity
        Shrieking with a fury of the insane
          At the sharp heartbreak tearing me in half
            Cutting off the golden cord to my freedom
            Which plunged me into a cage of steel
            Where I elected to live
              For a thousand horrid nights

Yet always my arm
  Was pinched between the bars
    Reaching for the gilded key
      That would unlock the tyranny of my mind
      Free me from my self-made prison
        Until finally sovereignty was revealed
        When I beheld her luminance
          Through the welcome eyes of clemency
            And the long-awaited savior of forgiveness
          Arrived once more

With that revered thought
  Pulsing through my emancipated veins
    I was again freed of the demon's bondage
      The teakettle swiftly sounded
        Its horn of celebration
          As one additional helium balloon
            Was placed in my expanding bundle

I remember the crucible of my life being enflamed
  By the dagger of jealousy
    I thrust at my brother
      Considering his achievements equated to mine
        Watching this venom poison my heart
          With another season of placing my life
            In the demon's shackles

The meandering road to acceptance
  Teemed with a mound of obstacles
    Forces detained me inside a tunnel to nowhere
      Blinding me to the clear path forward
        Or the manner to loose the bindings

Yet with the patient kiss of time
  Iniquity's persuasions were disabled
    My heart overflowed its love caress
      Surrendering this petrified illusion
        And the teakettle sang its hymn of liberty
          As one more helium balloon
            Enlarged my bouquet

I remember the kettle roasting for decades
  As my body was steadily draped in burden
    With the constricting chains
      Of some mysterious affliction
        Cutting off my lifeline to intended destiny
          As grief sliced all hope into pieces
            And anger tossed me like a wild tornado

Yet step by step
  I attempted to ascend
    The arduous stairway
      That would lead me to renewal
        Healing the abyss within my *Soul*
          Sanctioning wounds to mend
            While the arrows of my exodus
              Pointed me to an indisputable target

And there it was - forever reeling me in
  With the attraction of a thousand lodestones
    The recovery of my immortal diamond
      Victoriously embracing the perfection of it all
        In absolute love with everything
          Immaculately grateful for the fullness of what is

Could it have been
　A most authentic Thought
　　Of Love - of Perfection - of Unity?
　　　Could it have been
　　　　A maximum immersion into that Thought?
　　　　A Thought of no distance
　　　　　Between Limitless Love - and demon
　　　　No separation
　　　　　Between Absolute Perfection -
　　　　　　And every drama within my world

For there is only "one true Thought"
　And I aligned with It
　　Until I became the Thought
　　And the Thought was *All That Is*


- - - - - - - - -


Then the entire world
　Hummed through the teakettle's whistle
　　As it played its impeccable song once again
　　　Increasing the medley of my balloons
　　　With yet one more

A child who clings
　To a handful of helium balloons
　　Will discover that if someone
　　　Is constantly handing the child
　　　Additional balloons
　　　　One - after another - after another
　　　　　There will be an extraordinary moment
　　　　　When it will require
　　　　　　Just one more helium balloon
　　　　　　To lift the child's feet
　　　　　　　Off the ground

In order to victoriously soar
  Through this doorway
    Of unlimited promise
      Through this portal
        Of infinite possibility
          Through this stargate
            Of boundless emergence
              Is there one more thought of forgiveness
                One more embrace of acceptance
                One more act of kindness
                One more gift of love
                  That I am to offer?

Or maybe
  I have already burst from my cocoon
    And transformed into a butterfly
      My steaming kettle of life
        Has already sounded its triumphant whistle
        And my feet
          Have already lifted into the heavens

## Introduction to the Poem – _Are You - The Great Radiance?_

THIS POEM WAS INSPIRED by Andrew Cohen's book, _Evolutionary Enlightenment_. During the first few chapters of his book, Andrew proposed that the Big Bang, or what I sometimes poetically call "The Great Radiance", which initially burst forth at the beginning of time - and gave phenomenal form to our Universe, is even now energetically and physically taking place. Evolutionary science has evidentially demonstrated through astronomic observation that the massive explosion of energy at the origin of the Cosmos has been continually unfolding for the last 13.8 billion years. And this immense movement of energy is still unfolding at this very moment in time.

All of life is the natural consequence of this perpetually explosive energy - and all manifested forms are its diverse expressions of creativity. Furthermore, one of its most evolved and leading-edge expressions is currently being manifested through the awakened realizations of conscious self-reflective humans.

After finishing Andrew's book, I spent the next day contemplating his main evolutionary themes for many hours at the creek near my home. During my contemplation, I received the basic concept for a poem which had to do with the ever-unfolding continuous nature of the Big Bang. So, I began to write down a sketchy outline of what the poem was about - with the idea I would creatively develop it more formally at some time in the future.

Yet as I wrote the outline in my notebook, the whole poem seemed to magically appear very quickly in its fundamental entirety. I jotted down what was being given to me from some silent muse within.

Maybe it was the voice of the Big Bang coming through me - as I believe this cosmic voice perpetually comes through each of us in its unique and innovative ways - when we take time to become quiet and listen.

✳   ✳   ✳   ✳

# Circle of the Primary Stages of Evolution

**THE STAGE
OF CONSCIOUS
HUMAN LIFE**
THE DEVELOPMENT
OF BEINGS WITH SELF-
REFLECTIVE MINDS AND
COMPASSIONATE HEARTS
THAT ARE AWARE
OF THEIR OWN EVOLUTION

**THE STAGE
OF GALAXIES
TO PLANETS**
THE EARLY FORMATION
OF MASSIVE GALAXIES
WITH EXPLODING STARS
THAT CREATED PLANETS
WHERE PRIME ELEMENTS
WERE THE BASIS FOR LIFE

**THE STAGE
OF INTELLIGENT
LIFE FORMS**
SOME LIFE FORMS EVOLVE
COMPLEX EMOTIONS AND
THOUGHT PROCESSES,
RESPONDING TO IMPULSES
TO EXPAND AND EXPRESS
INDIVIDUAL POTENTIAL

**THE STAGE
OF BIOLOGICAL LIFE**
THE EMERGENCE
OF BIOLOGICAL LIFE
ON EARTH - PRODUCING
A RICH BIO-DIVERSITY
OF THE MYRIAD FORMS
OF PLANTS AND ANIMALS

# Are You - The Great Radiance?

A hundred billion turnings of winter - long ago
Well before the turbulent forces
That forged such creatures
As planets and moons
Before the gradual coalescing
Of stable central suns
Fashioned from the spray
Of shimmering supernovas
Before the dense assemblage
Of huge galactic clusters
Arising from colossal gaseous clouds
Of merging hydrogen atoms

There flashed an incomprehensibly massive burst
A hallowed instantaneous explosion
From a single point of luminosity
The initial fractal emergence of our entirety
Birthed from *the Radical Intelligence*
Within The Great Radiance
A big bang of thunderous surging
Contained within *Unbounded Silence*

Yet there seemed to be no one around
To hear the tumultuous boom of celestial rumbling
That placed our existence of unbridled potential
Into ceaseless motion -
Or was there?

Have you and I always been effulgent timeless beings
Standing in the hub of eternity
And now transmuted into stardust walking upright
Listening to the perpetual explosions of spaciousness
From our tiny thrones in the endless fields of forever?

Did this ancestral eruption
    Take place fourteen billion years ago?
        Or is its spatial music perhaps continuing to sound
            Right now in this incessant moment
                As the rhythm of a distant pulsar
                As the cry of a seagull
                    As a Mozart symphony?

Is its capricious mounting energy still unraveling
    Prospering like an ever-unfurling lotus flower
        Within a garden of unconstrained possibility?

And maybe you are its most recent bloom
    Offering the unique tones and hues
        Of your delicate petals
            As integral facets
                Of the immanent hands of the Cosmos
                As you yearn to blossom
                    Into a more glorious future

# Introduction to the Poem – *The Illusionist*

A LOT OF PEOPLE in OUR MODERN SOCIETY seem to be ensnared by an illusory and addictive notion that mechanically encourages them to desire things which have little value to a meaningful life. For example - the obsessive need to buy the next bigger house or latest popular car, to purchase the newest technological gadgets, to acquire the most recent exorbitant whims touted by the advertising industry, or to procure inconsequential and meaningless fads.

Sometimes this may occur if we find we're not thinking for ourselves. For it can be easy to get caught up in a compulsive societal mindset that's culturally accepted by the media, the general public, and most of the people around us. If we are not taught when we're young to think for ourselves - and to learn discernment and critical thinking, then we may get swept up in the river of illusion that much of the world is now trapped in.

Yet for some people there comes a sacred time when the conditions of life eventually motivate them to ask, "the Big Questions". This is a time to go deeper into self-reflection about what is undeniably true - and to explore ways to consciously experience a life of significance. And for many, a life of significance is a life that's in service to others.

When this type of inquiry occurs, a person may investigate specific existential questions - such as:  **What is my life truly about? - What really matters? - Why am I here? - Who am I?** These are the kind of questions which point one to the discovery of purpose, meaning, mission, and one's *True Nature*.

This poem was written as if the accepted beliefs and programming of an unconscious society is seen as "a performing magician" who enjoys tricking us into believing that certain illusions of the mind are true. When we learn that we're being tricked by a deceptive societal mindset - wake up from our sleep within the alluring dream - and break out of this mesmerizing collective hallucination, we can then free ourselves to courageously create our own reality, to realize why we're actually here in this life experience - and to discover who we really are.

✳   ✳   ✳   ✳

# Circle of Illusions of the Mind

## I AM MY BODY

THERE IS AN ILLUSION IN WHICH I BELIEVE I AM MY THOUGHTS, EMOTIONS, AND BODILY SENSATIONS RATHER THAN EXPERIENCING MY *TRUE NATURE* AS AN ENDLESS *RIVER OF AWARENESS* IN *A FIELD OF ONENESS*

## I AM ISOLATED

THERE IS AN ILLUSION IN WHICH I BELIEVE I AM MERELY AN ISOLATED BODY RATHER THAN MY *ETERNAL SELF* WHICH, THRU A CO-CREATION WITH *THE SOURCE OF LIFE,* BROUGHT MY BODY INTO MANIFESTED FORM

## I AM SEPARATE

THERE IS AN ILLUSION IN WHICH I BELIEVE I AM SEPARATE FROM THE REST OF CREATION RATHER THAN REALIZING "I *AM* THE UNIVERSE" AND THAT I'M ONE WITH EVERY FACET OF IT

## I AM NOT ENOUGH

THERE IS AN ILLUSION IN WHICH I BELIEVE I AM A PERSON THAT'S INADE-QUATE WHO MUST PROVE MY WORTHINESS RATHER THAN RECOGNIZING I AM, AND HAVE ALWAYS BEEN, THE MAGNIFICENCE OF *LIMITLESS LOVE*

# The Illusionist

He parades confidently
  Onto the cobalt blue stage
    His long black and scarlet trimmed cape
     Trailing behind him
      Like a dark wavering shadow
       Stalking in the wind
        Mimicking his audacious stride

The aroused audience
  Is poised in explosive anticipation
    Awaiting this flamboyant impresario
     To unleash his enchanted designs of trickery
    His slippery feats of illusion

His charismatic virtuosity
  Stemmed from an ancient family lineage
   The long track of seasoned illusionists
   That hailed before his reign
    Ancestors who poured into him
     Every magical ruse he mustered
    To advance the arcane craft
      Of sculpting fictional deceptions

He fervently devoted an entire life
To honing this Machiavellian art
  Now spending his days
   Carving the absolute
   Into trivial pieces
    The transcendent
     Into a gaudy carnival
      Mesmerizing thrilled spectators
       With his fabricated displays of fantasy

With masterful artistry he launches his first magic trick
Extracting an adorable white rabbit
From his allegedly empty black hat
Conjuring a captivated audience into the illusion
That the vast throng of existence
Is just a mere assemblage
Of countless discrete articles
A meager collection of furry animals
And some intriguing hats
And innumerable other isolated objects
Rather than - it is one unified infinite sea
Of effulgent energy in perpetual motion
Dancing through endless space

And the people clap furiously
Rejoicing with awe at his outrageous wizardry

For his next illusion he boldly stands
Within a tall coffin-shaped crimson box
Then suddenly vanishes with an extravagant flare
Dissolving into a fatal spaciousness
Artfully fooling the crowd
With his spellbinding trickery
Into believing that who and what he really is
Is a mere physical totality
Of all the microscopic cells within his material body
Which could evaporate into oblivion
At any lethal instant

His abrupt disappearance creates a deceptive ploy
That his mortal flesh is the entire sum of his identity
Charming his flock into a devious notion
That he's just an array of solid ingredients
Confined within the prison of his carnal frame
Rather than - who he truly is
Is an eternal limitless presence
Within a river of unbounded awareness

And the crowd roars vivaciously
  At his haunting exhibition

Afterward with clever pageantry
  He saws in half a scantily clothed woman
    Who cheerfully lies within a cryptic wooden tomb
     Entrancing his audience into the cunning illusion
      That the intrinsic feminine force
       Can be completely separated within a fractured world
       Severed from the innate masculine
        Obliviously torn from the sublimely consecrated
        Disconnected from the natural communion
       Within everything that's true
        Rather than - realizing they have always been
       Dual perfectly paired influences
      Abiding in flawless balance
        Like two intertwined Tango dancers
        Soaring in seamless harmony

And the onlookers all boisterously
  Applaud his riveting fantasy

He then dazzles the crowd with another illusion
  Submerging himself in a massive tank of water
    With his hands and feet bound tight
    While somehow shrewdly escaping his deceitful drama
    As he tricks a gullible congregation into believing
    That he - the Illusionist - was immersed
    In a solitary aquatic chamber
     Utterly divorced from *the Most Essential Ocean*
     Rather than - recognizing he's always been one
     With *the Ubiquitous Fullness of Everything*
     *The Absolute Source*
      *And Supreme Oceanic of All Life*

And the people scream
  In frenzied delight

He begins to introduce his fifth illusion
   Designed to explore the quantum reality of time
     When unexpectedly
       A loud disruptive bell
         Clamors repeatedly and obnoxiously
           Until with a harsh slap of his hand
             He shuts off a nearby alarm clock

The Illusionist shockingly discovers
   He is groggily at home
     Lying in his bed
       Rousing from his evening's reverie
         Realizing it's the renewed surprise
        Of morning once again
           The routine moment of unwrapping one's eyes
          To the swirl of a fresh new day

The ultimate time
   When all tricks of illusion
     From the scores of one's childish dreams
       Have inexplicably disappeared
         Faded with the hallucinations
           Of night's fantasies
         Like a ghostly fog
           On a still mirrored lake
             The way most illusive dreams evaporate
           When one is vividly awake

# Introduction to the Poem – _When I Dive Into The Stargate_

THIS POEM WAS WRITTEN AS AN EXPLORATION regarding the transcendent experience of self-love. There are some people who think "love" is an aspect of reality that only humans experience - and the rest of sentient life on Earth does not.

Some may also believe that "loving oneself" is an experience which is only felt within their own heart and mind - rather than experiencing "loving oneself" as a collective experience that all of humanity feels on some level.

Yet could this really be? Could it be that the experience of "self-love" is so much larger than we think or can imagine?

Could it be that to truly "love oneself" is to actually love every person on the planet - just the way they are without judgment?

Could it be that to truly "love oneself" is really about authentically loving every creature upon the Earth?

Could it be that to truly "love oneself" is about unconditionally loving every facet of reality within our life?

Let's see where this exploration takes us.

✳    ✳    ✳    ✳

# Circle of the Pillars of Self-Love
## (In Relation to the Pillars of Awakening)

**ONENESS**
I AM LOVING MYSELF
EVERY TIME
I FEEL INTERCONNECTED
AND ONE
WITH ALL OF
THE MYRIAD CREATIONS
OF THE WORLD

**GRATITUDE**
I AM LOVING MYSELF
EVERY TIME
I FEEL GRATEFUL
FOR WHAT
I'M LEARNING
FROM EACH EXPERIENCE
OF MY LIFE

**ACCEPTANCE**
I AM LOVING MYSELF
EVERY TIME
I ACCEPT
THAT MY LIFE
IS UNFOLDING
PERFECTLY
JUST AS IT IS

**SURRENDER**
I AM LOVING MYSELF
EVERY TIME
I LET GO
OF MY ATTACHMENTS
AND SURRENDER
EVERYTHING IN MY LIFE
TO *A GREATER POWER*

# When I Dive Into The Stargate

Today the Earth revealed to the Sun
  "I love who I am"
    For the spinning blue pearl felt warmly caressed
     By the resplendent radiance of its stellar orb
    Who responded "I know who you are"

Concurrently both the Sun and Earth
  Sprang forth within time's arrow
    Evolving as two dancers in symbiotic choreography
     Sculpting their supernova designs
      From the same colossal explosion
       Which formed a fiery solar core of luminous heat
        As well as a surging wheel of orbiting rocky fragments
        Spheres spinning round the furnace of a central hub

The arc of time chiseled lesser fragments into asteroids
  Until vigorous collisions of asteroids shaped planets
    Inserting one earthen ball into the sweet spot
     A perfect distance from all favors of the Sun
      A poised locality - not too frigid - nor overly searing

As the nuclear cauldron of its flaming solar sphere
  Churned into critical intensity
    The Earth replied by forming a titanic magnetic field
     To protect its fragile biotic children
      From the piercing glitter of its stellar blaze

In time the Sun's inferno grew ferocious
  Yet Earth tailored with adaptations
    To these mutable episodes
     Adorning itself in a gauzy cloak of atmosphere
      Modifying to the Sun's revisions
       As two dancers shuffling in perfect stride

The Sun hurled countless beams of shimmering photons
   To the greening shores of its partner
      While the Earth replied
         Producing a verdant harvest of abundance

Through merely the eyes of the mind
   And one's current science-based vantage
      This cosmological homeostasis of Earth and Sun
         Reigns as the ubiquitous natural law of the Cosmos

Yet when I dive into the Stargate
   The dimensional portal leading to fissures in my awareness
      Where I perceive Sun and Earth
         From the hallowed eyes of the heart
            I witness an intimate transcendent union
               A communion of two lovers immersed in celestial bliss
            Entwined within a blazing love
               In an embrace of perpetual devotion
            As each lover dances
               With the fervent movements of the other

The endless river of a billion seasons
   Were vital for flowers to secure their present shape
      Morphing - shifting - adapting
         To their fluid environment
            Merging with a crafty clan of bees
               That found means to bond in a cooperative ballet
               Of mutual dependence and collective advantage

Nomadic bees craved pollen from stationary flowers
   Flowers yearned for bees to proliferate species
      Marrying in clever ways partners had never fused

Merely through the eyes of the mind
   And one's biology-based vantage
      The woven interaction of these diverse creatures
         Emerged to further the planet's ecological tapestry

Yet when I dive into the Stargate
    Where I perceive the reveling of flowers and bees
      From the hallowed eyes of the heart
        There's a joining of two beloveds
          Beaming forth in unrestrained love
            An interweaving of ardent alliance
              Of two souls in euphoric communion
              Playing mutually as lovers do
                Enraptured in one another's grace

When I look at you
    I commonly fall into a bridled notion of reality
      Where I believe you're over there
        And I'm over here
          Encapsulated in these carbon-based shells
          Of replicating cells
            Delicately carved tissues
              And rivers of blood-drenched veins

A notion where stage and props are set
    For you and I to act out our epic sagas
      Of obsession and control
        Of triumph
          Of heroic gallantry
            Of gods against demons
              That might surface in the next scene
                Through varied characters we play
              Within an ever-unfolding drama

Yet when I dive into the Stargate
    Where I perceive you and me
      From the hallowed eyes of the heart
        We are two lovers merged as an Absolute
        Joined in the everlasting tenderness
        Of an enduring unity
          Dancing amid an unceasing flow of gratitude
          Within the field of mutual promise

From this sacramental temple
  Built upon time's infinite arrow
    Steering me toward the journey's zenith
      Where I encounter all that is holy and magnificent
        I can now proclaim
          "I love who I am"
            For who I am is you
              And every other audacious individual
                Exploring the far edges of unparalleled horizons
                Who boldly forge the future of our destiny

"I love who I am"
  For who I am is every flourishing petal
    Atop every dazzling flower stem
      On every life-rich pearl throughout the Cosmos
        Arranged within the sweet spot
          Of its central star

"I love who I am"
  For who I am is every Earth-like planet
    In adoring communion with its illuminated Sun
      Entwined in rapture with its exalted beloved

"I love who I am"
  For who I am is the delicious totality
    Of the entire banquet feast
      My capacity to fully taste and savor and digest
        Every wondrous and calamitous facet of life
          Just the way it is

# IV

# WINDOWS
# OF
# TRANSCENDENCE

# Introduction to the Poem - _The Mystical Blue_

THERE IS A NATURE SANCTUARY along the creek in Sedona that's very special to me. For over a decade, I would visit this sacred haven every week and spend about five hours of deep contemplation, meditation, and writing down my thoughts. This sanctuary is the hallowed location where many of my contemplative writings for JOURNEY OF THE GREAT CIRCLE originated.

One day as I was inwardly asking some existential questions and silently watching where my contemplations might take me, I was suddenly catapulted into an altered state of consciousness - a profound epiphany of awareness. All my senses became instantly heightened, and the sky seemed to explode into the most beautiful color of blue I have ever witnessed.

I felt a supreme Oneness with Nature - and with _Life_ - that was so overwhelming. It was as if I traveled through a dimensional threshold into a realm where everything shone with an intensified color spectrum. I wanted this transcendent experience to go on forever. However, it lasted about thirty to forty minutes - and eventually, my expanded awareness slowly returned to my normal state of consciousness.

Two weeks later I traveled to Telluride, Colorado, and hiked up to one of my favorite mountain waterfalls. There I took some creative time to anchor this amazing experience into a poem I call "The Mystical Blue".

✳    ✳    ✳    ✳

# The Mystical Blue

I have just caressed the magnificent
　That exalted transcendent estate
　　Which innocently requires my knees to tremble
　　My eyes to tear

I have by sheer mercy caught a sublime glimpse
　Of that which forever welcomes me
　　Eternally follows me
　　　Wherever I anchor my feet
　　　　Along this twisting rugged path
　　　　　Ceaselessly ascending
　　　　　　Toward my next horizon of ultimacy

Sometimes I flounder
　At times I triumph
　　Yet always carry this holiness everywhere
　　　This obscure doorway to consecrated worlds
　　　　This intangible portal to Eternity
　　　　This lofty threshold into Mystery

For most of my sundial's shadows
　This gateway appeared just out of reach
　　Somewhere slightly past the edge
　　　Scarcely beyond the range
　　　　Of my outstretched fingertips
　　　　Invisible - unfathomable

Yet on this bejeweled day
　From out of nowhere - or everywhere
　　It intoned a most intimate ancestral song
　　　As if I could hear
　　　　Fabled words within my *Soul*
　　　　　"I bid you to pierce my hallowed veil"

I stumbled upon a luminous treasure chest
Unlocked by ubiquitous grace
Satiating me with gems of ecstasy
As I fell into a rapturous vortex
Melting my bursting heart
Into tiny teardrops of gratitude
And pools of liquid remembrance

I suddenly found myself
At the Center of Everything
For I was both the midpoint of the circle
As well as the surface of the sphere

Could it be that the bewildering paradox
Of a numinous existential question
Can open extraordinary entries
Can crack the artificial veils
Of illusory separation
And gather me into
An uncommon world of such Union?

Why am I here upon this terrestrial globe?
What in creation really matters?
Will I ever fathom what life is truly about?
Who am I?
And of course the incessant inquiry
Where is the elusive God?

These nascent questions
Refuse to render definitive answers
Yet a mere asking
Of such reality-shattering probes
Parted the chronic veil
The stone wall of my rigid beliefs
Revealing the Mystical Blue
Towering high above me

I turned my head toward the azure sky
  There it was parading before me
    The heavens erupting in mesmerizing radiance
      With the pristine fullness of a limitless Blue
        Yet such vivid stunning color
          These eyes had never beheld

It dazzled me with wonderment
  It rattled me to the core with its supernal essence
    It whispered to me
      How holy I am - how eternal - how infinitely loved
      And I believed
        I knew - I cried

Shaken by this momentary miracle
  I was unexpectedly lifted to a revered shrine
    As the fingers of God etched into my memory
      A glance of rapturous forever
        Where I danced in sovereignty
          As the primal potency in everything

But then - as I witnessed myself take another breath
  The Kiss of Eternity began to slip away
    The perpetual stream of time
      Returned to unfurl its banner
        The river of change started to surge once again

The Mystical Blue that hung in the firmament
  Like an ephemeral masterpiece
    Was inexplicably rendered anew
      Was restored to more muted tones
        An austere pallid sky
          Covered with brushstrokes
            Of a soundless cobalt tint
            A common secular color
              From the customary spectrum
                Of my commonplace hues

The Mystical Blue gently melted away
  Steadily evaporated
    Then was gone
      And I sighed

Still I stand with bold certainty
  This sanctified gateway into Mystery
    This ecstatic portal of grace
      Journeys within me wherever I wander
        Is constantly kissing my cheek
          And at times
            Is just beyond
              The sharp edge of my sight

So each day I seize its invitation
  I listen for another of its countless songs
    I dance and breathe to remain present
      To stay aligned with the Mystery
        To wait patiently so I may be ushered
          Toward my next horizon of possibility
            And I humbly continue to ask questions

# Introduction to the Poem - _The Great Story Of Perfection_

I WAS CAMPING IN A WILDERNESS SITE on the banks of Lake Pleasant near Phoenix, Arizona in early spring, enjoying the lush vernal flowers and the desert's sublime silence. One morning I began to contemplate the grand celestial story of astronomy - or what I and others call "The Great Story of the Universe". This led me to observing and celebrating (at least from the wide lens of a Big Picture perspective) that 13.8 billion years of cosmological and planetary evolution have been unfolding absolutely perfect. Galaxies, stars, planets, oceans, volcanos, myriad life forms - all evolving and unfolding perfectly.

Yet I - in this perfectly evolved human body and cognitively programmed by many of humanity's collective convictions, have lived most of my life with the common belief that, in my everyday experience, reality does not always unfold perfectly for me. In my life like most of us, there have been many difficult challenges and unpleasant disturbances that do not feel perfect. What happened when humans came upon the evolutionary scene? Did the Great Cosmic Design of the Universe, somehow, get off track?

This poem explores the idea that all of humanity - and all of life, including you and me, is a never-ending continuation of the infinite perfection that has always been taking place within the Universe.

I will also note - this poem was written with the assumption that we live in a hypothetical "multiverse". A multiverse is a theoretical concept in advanced physics stating that our massive universe is only one universe of many universes throughout existence. In the multiverse, all universes co-exist together within one vast Unified Field - or Field of Infinite Intelligence - much like many individual biological cells co-exist together within one organism.

\* \* \* \*

# The Great Story Of Perfection

Peering through the omniscient eyes of *The Great Mystery*
　I watch the endless cosmic dance
　　Of an emergence of colossal Universes
　　　Each a diverse magnitude and shape
　　　　With unique faces and physiques
　　　　　All exploding into common existence
　　　　　　As they vigorously nudge into one another

Each in time disappears into spaciousness
　Transfiguring from a gargantuan being into non-being
　　While I victoriously celebrate
　　　That this ceaseless transmutation of the multiverse
　　　　Can only be part of the perfection

From the almighty eyes of *The Great I Am*
　I witness the massive blossoming
　　Of my provincial Universe
　　　Constantly unfolding its enormous petals
　　　　Its billions of star-drenched galaxies
　　　　　As each galactic flower petal
　　　　　　Steadily opens to the celestial enigma
　　　　　　　While I rejoice that its vast mystical beauty
　　　　　　　Can only be part of the perfection

Within the supreme eyes of *The Great Spirit*
　I monitor the incessant turning
　　Of this milky spiral Galaxy
　　　That tenderly enfolds me
　　　　Cradling me with its countless solar orbs
　　　　　Bathing me in its astral symphony
　　　　　　Of light and shadow
　　　　　　　While I delight that its luminous exaltation
　　　　　　　Can only be part of the perfection

Gazing through the all-seeing eyes of *Great Father Sun*
    I perceive the vigorous tapestry
        Of chiseled planets orbiting through space
            Around a golden fire ball
                Throwing spears of blazing rays
                At spherical moving targets
                    While I revel that this circumnavigating of the wheel
                    Within such a sublime system
                        Can only be part of the perfection

From the all-merciful eyes of *Great Mother Earth*
    I view a seemingly insignificant blue and white pearl
        Unpretentiously turning on its terrestrial axis
            Enjoying the sweet spot within the Sun's glow
                Enabling its jungles - deserts - mountains - oceans
                To flourish with an unfathomable spark of life
                    While I celebrate the rich diversity of heaven's garden
                    Can only be part of the perfection

Within the womb of the *Mother*
    Impregnated with the seed of the *Father*
        Emerges the sons and daughters of *the Infinite One*

The progeny now conscious and clever enough
    To gaze into haunting telescopes
        And mesmerizing microscopes
            To recognize something spectacular
            To peer across the lens of the *Soul*
                Reflecting the mirror of *The True Self*

A mirror that speaks to every set of eyes
    Displaying one's magnificence
        One's superb luminosity
            One's jeweled radiance
            One's unclaimed destiny
                Yet in order to see
                    One must glance unwaveringly into its refection

So now with eyes wide open
  To the elegant musings of existence
    Is there still anyone upon the planet
      Who is arrogant enough to proclaim
        That the Universe of quantum possibilities
          Which right now is exploding within their heart
            As well as everything orbiting within their life
              Is not being expressed in a most miraculous manner
                As an exquisitely flawless enterprise

A manner that - yes - can only be seen
  As part of an absolute perfection
    As part of a perfect Universe
      As part of a perfect world
        That has immaculately created a perfect you
          And maybe a few disbelieving arrogant rebels

# Introduction to the Poem - _Oneness – A Sea Of Luminosity_

IN THE SUMMER OF 2017, I experienced the sublime gift of an altered state of consciousness at a healing gathering taking place within a circle of large pine trees. During this extended period of exalted epiphany, I received an extraordinary glimpse of Oneness while I was talking with a friend. As I looked at his face and body, they appeared separate and distinct from me - in the way most objects and people seem separate and distinct within the "normal" perception of my everyday world.

Yet when I closed my eyes, I saw the illuminated outline of his face and body framed within "a sea of exquisitely brilliant and mesmerizing light." Furthermore, the entire physical environment around him was made up of that same radiant light.

As I reveled within my internal realm with eyes shut, I perceived that my arm was also pulsating with that same luminance - as was everything around me. All the myriad light frequencies were connected as one interwoven ocean of luminosity, even though I could "perceive" subtle defining boundaries of specific images - like my friend's body, my arm, the garden chairs, and the surrounding trees.

Every time I opened my eyes, I saw the apparent vision of my external world as illusory images of separation. Yet when I again closed my eyes, I perceived the Oneness of _an infinite field of radiance._

Bats, dolphins, bees, butterflies, and many other life forms view the physical world through their eyes in a way much different than we humans do. These animals see their exterior world through a different slice of the full electromagnetic frequencies than we do. Therefore, they see things a little differently.

Could we one day learn to observe the luminous world of electromagnetic possibility like they do - and perceive much more of the myriad frequencies that exist, but can't yet see?

Here is the poem I wrote about this transcendent experience.

✳    ✳    ✳    ✳

# Oneness – A Sea Of Luminosity

My friend's eyes burned with excitement
As he apprised me of a stunning documentary
Displaying buoyant promises for this emergent world
Decreeing at this present season
The way humans are sculpting their lives
Appears to be upside down and inside out

The film's assertion predicted a restored global vision
A pinnacle view of willfully seizing the reins
Deliberately becoming a commanding overseer
Of our own mutable screenplay

So I entered the theater with aroused anticipation
Settling in my seat as the show began
It wasn't like anything I've witnessed before
It invited me to envision a resurrected planet
I was urged to partake in its unfolding
It pleaded with me to picture limitless possibility

The narrator's firm voice beckoned with authority
To imagine a spacious mighty ocean
To dream of my existence as a wave within immensity
To know that my friends - family - every person I knew
Sailed as a superior ripple in an unbounded sea
Where we artfully navigated its majesty

All my heart-centered training
Prepared me for this arcane allegory
My awareness hovered in its acute significance
Within the silent canyons of a seeker's mind
Yet my *Soul* had not yet tasted
The absolute feast of this knowing
So I lingered patiently at the banquet table

The narrator summoned me to close my eyes
I saw each wave crest within me - then disappear again
As dazzled points of spectral brilliance
Breakers dancing upon a jeweled ocean
A field of moments contained within a diamond's glow
Merged with voluminous sprays of illumination
In some mesmerizing choreography of mystery

The film's brazen voice
Bid me to open my eyes
Where I beheld relentless swells and troughs
Of heroic cobalt blue waters
Emerging triumphantly
Within a briny sea

Again commanded to close my eyes
The oceanic panorama lingered
Yet only as a sparkling feast of luminosity
Igniting the vision of my innermost mindscape

The film roused me with open eyes
To envision a titanic infinite shoreline
A white sandy beach
With no discernable edges
To imagine being a distinct grain of sand
One magnificent creation amid this eternal shore
And that every person who danced with me
Was also a unique speck of universe
As we whirled together to the stellar music
In a benevolent embrace of communion

Once more the voice beckoned to close my eyes
The inner shoreline became iridescent starlight
I saw each grain as an explosion of radiance
Blazing fireworks burst within me
Particles of sand became beams interwoven
Across a glittering beach without boundaries

I opened my eyes yet again
  To a scene of an immaculate cosmic shoreline
    Touching a galactic unbounded sea

I closed my eyes to examine anew
  The ferocious interlacing light
    With its interminable spectral hues
      Satiating the innermost chambers of my heart

The next time my eyes opened
  The movie concluded
    It required quite some time
      To conjure the potency to stand
        Precariously parade out of the theater
          Out amidst the pulsing order and chaos of a day

The first thing I witnessed in this pristine world - was you
  In your holiness and magnificence
    As you have always truly been
      The glory of your Fully Perfected Self
        The supreme majesty of your Limitless Nature

It was so natural to close my eyes
  To celebrate the supernal shimmer of your love light
    The luminous verity of who you really are

At last my eyes opened to the fullness
  With a burning desire to ask a question
    "Would you trust me to take you somewhere
      Somewhere exceptional
        For there's a stunning documentary
          I want you to experience?"

You smiled as if full of prescience
  Then knowingly your face lit up
    Certain that everything is a sea of luminosity
      As you simply closed your eyes

# The Edge

A haunting twilight shimmers
  The day's stabbing sunlight has nearly vanished
    Evening's glacial starshine has not yet come
      Here I glide into the rapturous air of silence

Stillness is where I deftly ride
  Navigating the sharp edge of mystery
    Somewhere between a luminous beam of transparency
      And a tender shadow of obscurity
        A transcendent midpoint
          Where I neither hold on - nor let go

In this place of my surrendered heart
  I stride as if treading upon one scantily thin strand
    Within an invisible spider's web
      Separating these dual complimentary worlds

On the edge - there is nowhere to go
  Yet I navigate each hallowed commencement - or finality
    With the inferno of my zeal
      On a point - there is nothing to do
        Yet these creative arms ceaselessly yearn
          To sculpt further arcs of beauty

Everything I experience as *Life* - constantly petitions
  That another bridge be fashioned
    Which has already been imagined
      Spanning these two vast universes
        Transporting me from anguish to renewal
          From the fragmentation of time
            To the tranquility of wholeness
              From an explosion of duplicity
                To the supremacy of One

Within the sublime stillness
Of the *All* that never changes
I am catapulted back one more time
Into a field of discovery and wonder
Amidst the relentless dance
Of this ostensible paradox
Plunged into profound gratitude
That this audacious journey
Has escorted me once again
To the razor's edge

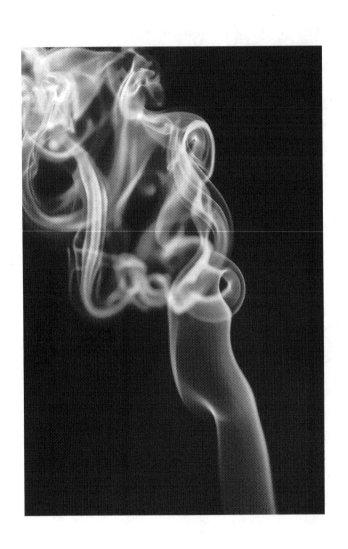

# Chalice Of The *Soul*

Can a *Soul* be savored like vintage wine
    Delicately poured into the chalice of carnal experience
      Cascading from spaciousness
        Into life's crystal goblet
          And relished like a sweet ale?

Some metaphysicians of modern religiosity
    Stand with authoritative posture
      Behind carved wooden lecterns
        Declaring the ever-advancing Cosmos
          Including all we glimpse or touch
            Flared forth out of untainted nothingness
          From the Unbounded Heart of God

Likewise present-day priests
    Of quantum mechanics
      Preach their holy sermons
        On the sacrament of "enlightened alchemy"
        Heralding how sub-atomic particles
          Miraculously emerged into solid forms
        From the invisible raptures
          Of a dimensionless *Unified Field*
            The habitat of a resplendent void

And even some contemporary evolutionaries
    Claim an assortment of philosophies
      They are the scholastic midwives
        Speculating that every unseen *Soul*
        Is birthed from *One Great Soul*
          From which the novel shapes of visceral bodies
          Are meticulously chiseled into existence
        From the ubiquitous clay
          Of a *Unified Field*

The *Soul* is a master chalice maker
　　Ever fashioning the shifting terrestrial contours
　　　Of my present worldly vessel
　　　　So I can choose to fill it
　　　　　With either the aged wine of compassion
　　　　　Or the spoiled vinegar of fear

The *Soul* is akin to the sublime creator
　　Of a tiny yet burgeoning seed
　　　Placed within the fertile soil of Earth's garden
　　　　For me to nurture
　　　　　With either my escalating gratitude
　　　　　Or choke in the drought
　　　　　　Of my constrictive thoughts
　　　　　　Of not having enough

The *Soul* is like the seasoned builder
　　Of a finely crafted house
　　　Constructed so I may either abide within
　　　　Shrouded in harmony and reverence
　　　　　Or rant and rage
　　　　　　With chronic reams of discord

Expansive fruitful living
　　Or the gradual decay
　　　From unwanted contraction
　　　　Blossoming forth in abundant glory
　　　　　Or withering on the vine of delusion
　　　　　Soaring upward to sit upon
　　　　　　A throne of supernal stars
　　　　　　Or addictively imprisoned
　　　　　　　In my self-imposed cage

How many of my life adventures
　　That I hold in the caress of my heart
　　　Are sculpted
　　　　By the *Soul's* visionary hand?

Yet how much do I shape or alter myself
  With every thought I cradle
    Every action I seize
      Along the countless forks in the road
        Where my journey
          Can bolt either right or left
            Up or down
              Forwards or backwards
                With my candid choices
                  To embrace *Love*
                    Or not?

The *Soul* has always been
  The eternal artist of the invisible
    With buoyant visions
      Of a more celebrated future

Each day as the fiery sun dawns
  I claim the hallowed opportunity
    To manifest its magnificent prophecies
      To be the creator of its revelatory dreams
        To make its sacred art visible
          To savor its vintage wine

# Life After Death

It is staggeringly evident
   That you're stalking me
      You are there reeling me in
         Whatever pathway I scurry
        Always treading closer
           With every ephemeral twilight
         As each fleeting day
            Melts into another - then another

In the marrow of my bones
   Something knew this hour would come
      The fruit of time has ripened
     I have suffered enough
        Displayed these scars sufficiently
          Now the battle to control - to conquer
        Has irreversibly waned
       I offer gratitude instead
           Merged with a herculean concession
         To what is soon inescapable

And still you approach
   So I lay my self upon the funeral pyre
      Returning identity to its all-consuming flames
        Surrendering every attachment of my fragile image
       Willing to be transmuted
      By your inevitable renovating
     Of my yielding heart

You move nearer still
   I fully accept this unavoidable destiny
      Relinquishing mortality's portal to the unknown
     Awaiting impending fate
      With humility and grace

I pivot my head to find you
   Now you're almost upon me
      So near that at last I recognize you
         The totality of awareness
            The embrace of liberty
               The cosmos of spaciousness
                  Peering through your eyes
                     As I gaze back at you

So close at hand
   That the veil is pierced
      The fog of illusion dissolved
         I have disappeared
            I cannot find my self anywhere
               Except where you are
                  Yet you are everywhere

The hunter must capture his prey
   Caterpillars must one day take wing
      Death of a crusty former self
         Must always blossom
            Into fresh fluid birth
               Life's promised renewal
                  Must forever and always unfold

Is all of humanity
   Ultimately destined for this?
      Of course
         There is no opposite to Life
            There can be no converse to Love's verity
               Sacred exploration must in due course
                  Lead to this
                     Oh what a glorious awakening

# V

# DOORWAYS
# TO
# IMAGINATION

# The Pillars Of The Temple Are Crumbling

The Babylonians - the Egyptians - the Greeks - the Hindus - the Mayans
   They each built them for their revered rituals
      Sculpted cylindrical towers and monolithic temples
      Reaching for the hidden edge of an endless sky

Ancient citadels embodying chiseled concepts
   Beliefs that once stood massive and indestructible
      Yet upon wheels of time
         Deteriorated into ruin
            Feebly crumbling into tiny fragments
            Giving way for the succeeding swell
               Of new ceremonial palaces to be assembled

Of course today everyone is building them
   You and me and they
      Beliefs are like thick rock-hewed pillars
         Buttressing a mighty temple
            Shoring up some novel perspective
         Currently in fashion

Yet amidst eons of frozen opinions
   And stagnant worldviews
      Hairline cracks appear
         In these seemingly solid structures
            Rigid pillars begin to break apart
               From ceaseless biting winds of renewal
               From the embryonic rumblings
                  Of a quaking earth hungering for rebirth

Once - our primeval world was construed
   To be a titanic flat surface
      Like a colossal piece of grey shale
         With oceanic waters halting at distant horizons

But the pillars of the temple began to crumble
  When brave astute sailors
    Maneuvered their wooden schooners
      Beyond the ocean's rationed edge
        Only to encounter a palpable spherical globe
          With an entirely new terrain
            Waiting on the other side of freedom

Once - our verdant planet was conceived
  To be the vital hub of the Cosmos
    The central heart of a star-filled firmament
      Of *All That Is* - or *Ever Was*

But the pillars of the temple began to crumble
  When dauntless explorers of midnight skies
    Revealed through the telescopic lens of possibility
      Our annual circumnavigation of the Sun
        Which itself orbits within a vast sphere
          Of neighboring solar systems
            Inside the swirl of a massive spiral galaxy
              That spins amid billions of galactic wonders

Once - we envisioned our frail temporal bodies
  As mere hard solid structures
    Uniformly dense resembling the sundry clays of earth
      For within the early bounds of perception
        That's all we were skilled enough to know

But the pillars of the temple began to crumble
  When vanguard physicists revealed
    Our fragile bodies
      And all earthen trinkets
        Are 99.99% empty space
          With just a few sub-atomic particles
            Dancing around at dizzying speeds
              Which have become visible
                Bursting out of a numinous void

Once - we considered all people
　　White - black - brown - yellow
　　　　Were categorically divergent from one another
　　　　So we conjured up stories to fear them
　　　　　With ghostly heroes and wicked villains
　　　　　　Imprisoning each uniquely hued creature
　　　　In their color-coded box

But the pillars of the temple began to crumble
　　When bold evolutionary scientists
　　　Demonstrated through DNA analysis
　　　We are all one united human family
　　　　That emerged from the woodlands
　　　　　Of a migrating tribe of primal Africans

Once - we conjured the thought
　　We were all separate from one another
　　That I was over here
　　　And you were over there
　　　　We seemed to float randomly
　　　　As individual isolated islands
　　　　　Disconnected upon a harsh raging sea
　　　　Of solitary experience

But the pillars of the temple began to crumble
　　When the daring geniuses of quantum mechanics
　　Proved all structures in the Universe
　　　Are intimately interconnected
　　　　As one unified field of energy
　　　　　One interwoven dance of existence
　　　　In ceaseless motion

Now - the time has come
　　When we must take yet another leap
　　Stretch the chambers of our hearts
　　　Prepare for the pillars of the temple
　　　To crumble once again

For when we fervently gaze out
　　Into the spacious silence of the Cosmos
　　　With unrestricted and unbridled eyes
　　　　We clearly perceive with exalted vision
　　　　　That not only - can we witness a colossal Universe
　　　　　　*The Supreme Fullness of All That Is*
　　　　　　But that unambiguously
　　　　　　　We are intimately one - with the Universe

Therefore - when we passionately look within
　　And severely gaze with naked abandonment
　　　With untainted vision and unshackled eyes
　　　　That not only - can we conclusively find our notion of God
　　　　　Since God is everywhere - is everything
　　　　　　And thus the *Eternal Absolute* is within you and me
　　　　　　But we can also discover - without doubt
　　　　　　　That literally - we *are* - the ultimate paradox
　　　　　　　　Which clearly implies - we *are* - everywhere

For in some unfathomable and incomprehensible way
　　Beyond the perpetual churnings of our simple minds
　　　Beyond our self-oriented images of grandeur
　　　　As the pillars of the temple crumble once again
　　　　　Could we dare ask ourselves -
　　　　　　Since nothing exists that is not God
　　　　　　　*The Totality of Everything* within our Universe
　　　　　　　Is it remotely possible
　　　　　　　　That we are both a part of the Universe
　　　　　　　　And we *are* the Universe
　　　　　　　　　At the same time?

# A Thundering Train Of Beliefs

An imperial eagle in flight
Towering high above
Terrestrial shapes and contours
Possesses a pinnacle vantage
As it examines far below
A thundering train
Steadily slithering across
Rails of dogmatic experience
Snaking a curvaceous path
Through an opinionated countryside

Every train of philosophy must advance across time
Allowing its vigilant passengers a buoyant chance
To restore the misdirected tracks
Of their lifetime storylines
To exchange obsolete scripts
For much nobler versions
Depending on where people ride
Within this epic train of mounting awareness

The lofty winged flyer
Must descend toward the advancing convoy
To hover near so as to listen in
On every novel parable
From each wanderer's personal saga

Avian ears glide swiftly over railcars
Scanning for travelers with rigid minds - unyielding hearts
Those who cling to antiquated beliefs
Yet still vaguely aware that their archaic doctrines
Yearn to morph into something fresh - progressive
To be one day tempered
With superior wisdom

Every mind holds a natural craving for renewal
An organic longing for one's train of thought
To transport outdated beliefs
Through a timeless threshold into the next horizon
To cross into another judicious season
Into an unexplored territory
Into an uncharted terrain of fresh possibilities
Journeying from dry desert - to lush forest
From dusty canyon - to fertile grassland

All trains of diverse politics
Have the sheer ache to forge ahead
From an ancient landscape to an expansive vista
So they may finally drink in
An entirely novel perspective
And other spacious points of view

Yet trains of abject rigidity
Must regularly stop
From prolonged periods of stringency
Parched with thirst
From the bondage of opinion
From the shadows of judgment
Until they enact a crucial refueling
At a nearby station

Beliefs have fostered
A thousand horrific years of Holy Wars
Have placed us softly
On the craterous dust of the Moon
And will at some point
Catapult us to a neighboring star

Beliefs have imprisoned slaves
And unshackled constellations of women
Have brutally tortured people to death
And dawned a promising vision of democracy

Scores of beliefs
   Are constantly putting people to sleep
     Yet merged with understanding
      Can awaken them

From where majestic eagles
  Consider the mortal world below
   The obsolescent inflexible mind
    Appears like a massive iceberg
     Floating randomly upon a vast epic sea
      In which only a small bundle of one's beliefs
     Rise above the water's surface
      Where they are readied for daily exploit

The greatest storehouse
  Of one's alleged truths
   Are inadvertently hidden
    Far below the surface of awareness
     Unconsciously maneuvering
      The ship of one's choices
       And mechanically steering
        The rudder of one's actions

Yet most travelers don't ride for very long
  Addictively compelled to depart the train
   At the nearest diverging station
    Remaining frozen in their notions
     In the unyielding ice of ignorance
      Rather than warming themselves
       In the endless intelligence of wisdom
        Through communion with perpetual sunlight

There can be a crusty hesitation
  About learning what's round a further turn of the track
   Which might ruffle the existing state of affairs
    If one was to welcome an embrace
     Of a whole new renovated vantage of the world

Only eagles in flight
  Ascending high enough
    Can gaze down to monitor
      The full spectrum storyline
        Of one who yearns to ride a freedom train
          Where they catch sight
            Of all that's luminous and superb

A true train of freedom
  Carries eager open minds
    Over tracks of fresh experience
      Minds which were once static icebergs
        Yet now exploring life's limitless terrains
          Where riders have learned to dwell
            With an entirety of their beliefs
              Elevated above the depths
                Fully exposed
                  To a most supernal light

The truly sanctified home
  Where all tracks of experience
    Ultimately lead
      Where only the holiest scripts are written
        The abode where life's most glorious saga
          Is played out on every liberated stage
            An impassioned place of believing
              In the supreme paradise
                That awaits within the core
                  Of every sovereign heart

# Evolution Of Miracles

At an early phase within primeval ages
Of humanity's extensive infancy
During those days of prehistoric moons
Long before the emergence of astute ancients
There existed no invention
Or pictorial word for "air"

Yet after the arduous turning of ample pages of time
I can now sail among multi-hued skies
In untethered balloon ships
Suspended like champagne bubbles
Floating upon air's density
By the miracle
Of some clever unseen magic

Humans then laboriously crawled
Through a chapter of adolescence
As grueling centuries flickered by
Evenings lit only with the silvery sparkle
Of dancing candles
Or heaven's occasional thunderbolt
To bring luminosity
To each of their steel black nights
Transforming nocturnal darkness
Into a tunnel of visibility

Yet today after the studies of countless ages
How could I have ever fathomed
That these flashing currents of the sky gods
Would one day be thrust through metal strands
To illuminate my twilight hours
With the luminous miracle
Of their invisible electric forces

Civilization then ripened
　Into a maturity of adulthood
　　Where apples sometimes plummet
　　From trees like arrows
　　　To arrive at their target
　　　Upon the minds of geniuses
　　　　Inspiring a new breed
　　　　Of mathematical paradigms
　　　　　That birthed an elegant scheme
　　　　Of physical laws
　　　　　Portraying the cosmic dance
　　　　Of earth and heaven
　　　　　An intricate numerical system
　　　　Left unchallenged
　　　　　For hundreds of mortal years

Yet now with further pages of history unfurled
　Another portal is cracked open
　　For when I peer into its quantum rabbit hole
　　I see a grander enlightened king of intellect
　　Has sat upon another throne of miracles
　　　With ideas that exploded into awareness
　　　With the acumen to split an atom
　　　　Offering power beyond imagination
　　　And terrors beyond belief

Now in the unfolding chain of my seasons
　The next of a ceaseless string of chapters
　　Within the hallowed book of life
　　I stand on a towering precipice
　　　With one foot again
　　　　Poised to catapult courageously
　　　Into the stars
　　　　The other desperately clutching
　　　　The solid security of rock

Could it be a gift
  That this mind doesn't yet understand
    Doesn't yet perceive the bigger picture
     The countless pathways
      Which can lead to healing
       The matrix of unknown journeys
      That's yet to be revealed
        The uncertainty of undiscovered frontiers
       That yearns to bring me wholeness
       And ever-advancing vibrancy?

Yes - I've been humbled before
  In this territory of timeworn beliefs
   Yet I must now cut a brand new trail
    Through the blinding dense brush
     Through the darkened jungle thickets
    Past the hidden doorway
     To a revered story of possibility
    And to yet another
      Of creation's limitless miracles

# The Imaginator

As the first shimmering light
   Of an effulgent new day
      Tenderly rubbed up against her dreamy eyes
         She opened them with a champion's excitement

She was enchanted that the morning's kiss of sunlight
   Caught a glimpse of her lucid imagination
      Viewing it as the *Soul's* architect
         Meant for creating new universes
            Knowing there had never been
               A flash of emergent possibility
                  Like this resplendent moment

She fathomed the enormous power
   Of an unwavering mind
      A wondrous force for building inventive worlds
         Recognizing she was a sculptor of ideas
            Able to fashion sub-atomic particles
               Into the illusory clay of life's majestic art
                  With the laser-like focus
                     Of her sharpened thoughts
                        And authentic passion

She understood how to elegantly unearth
   A treasure chest of miracles
      Humbly noticing that she is today
         Who yesterday she imagined she would be

Employing one of the supreme tools
   In her vast yet unpretentious toolbox
      She discovered an enigmatic key
         Which revealed to her
            That the forms and shapes of tomorrow
               Are what she fervently imagines today

She was now an alchemist of the elementals
   A sculptor of dreams
      An artist of visions
         A builder of imminent worlds

Now after the swelling light of the Sun
   Had leisurely ascended
      Into the cradle of the sky
         She had created her day

She was ready to cross the threshold
   Into the earthen playground
      Where she would join
         The other imaginators
            Who were eager to witness
               What works of genius would be fashioned
             By the skillful hands of Masters
               And the sacredness of an untethered Heart

# The Enigma Of A Philosophy

Cradle an arousing question
  "Do your philosophies exist forever?"

Defensively caged within the prison
  Of obsolescent beliefs
    The Earth was once perceived as the pious hub
      Of a colossal intergalactic wheel
        The sanctified center of the entire known universe
        The hallowed midpoint
          Of all that shimmers throughout the heavens

Yet academics employing the illumined marvel
  Of massive mountain-top telescopes
    Have now established our blue and white pearl
      Orbits a mid-size stellar luminary
        In the company of a titanic array
          Of celestial solar giants
            As part of countless galactic threads
              Weaving a most gargantuan universal tapestry

The terrestrial world was formerly alleged
  To be flat horizontal expanse
    Through the fledgling eyes of ancestors
      Claiming those who foolishly sailed schooners
        Beyond its fixed horizon
          Would plummet past the sharp edge of oceans
          To lose themselves amid a bonfire of stars

Yet their astute progeny dawned wiser skins
  Now ubiquitously navigating their proud aerial ships
    Which encircle the globe along spherical latitudes
      Exploiting the declaration that our planet
        Exhibits more than two spatial dimensions

Within the obstinate mansions
Of motley carnal intellects
Where the fraudulent illusion
Of security abides
The Cosmos was previously thought
To have a single obligatory origin
Bestowed by a cunning deity
Existing beyond the labyrinth of time
One immense explosive birth
Deprived of a mother's womb

Yet now a measure of prophetic wizards
From arcane cosmology
Declare that our mammoth fiery burst of reality
Is just a wondrous solitary drop
Within an eternal river
Of endless cosmic births
And celestial demises

Gazing into the whimsical thresholds
Of the many mortal sky dreams
One can observe
The apparent mystical
A leaf turns sunlight into energy
A cell turns nutrients into power
A mind turns imagination into form
Thought becomes the Eiffel Tower
A pepperoni pizza
Or an expedition to the moon

Still - there are endless multitudes
Of riveting enigmas
And bewildering riddles
That brains cannot position
Into pretty little organized boxes
Or neat tidy categories

No one yet fathoms
  How the conundrum of life sprang forth
    From the sweltering cauldrons of volcanic soup
      Or in what way amoebic single-celled creatures
        Morphed into mammalian opposites
          Of male and female
            Or how humans advanced
              To be propagators of linguistics
                While concocting the wild art of laughter
                  And certainly not the existential disclosure
                    Of how Creation
                      Mysteriously surged into being

Mystery lurks behind the solution
  To every unanswered question
    Unfamiliar magic delves at the core
      Of all inexplicable phenomena
        The unknown is the alchemical seed
          Of each original discovery

Maybe the question is not
  "Do your philosophies exist forever?"
    But might be phrased
      "Is it possible to find any philosophy
        In all of existence
          That does not ultimately revolutionize?"

✳

✳ · ✳

✳

# VI

# THRESHOLDS TO THE SACRED OTHER

# The Holiest Of All Chalices

Waiting at the heart of every universe
Lies the holiest of all chalices
The one that perpetually yearns
For the hand of the most absolute love
To retrieve a hallowed vessel
So a perfect nectar may be poured
Into its supreme cup

I am a vessel of ever emergent love
Eager to pour into your chalice
The melded exuberant wine
Of all that we are
And all we desire to be

Celebrating your benevolence
I drink from your regal grail
From the triumphant glorious
Of who and what you are
Cherishing the succulent taste
And velvety magnificence
Of our sacred vintage

This consecrated libation
Quenches my ancestral thirst for communion
With the majesty of your illumined eyes
The jubilation of your luminous being
The wisdom of your supernal smile

We are two adjoining wings
From the same celestial falcon
Wine merged with holy chalice
Love united with sovereign form

I exultantly drink
　　All that I am offered
　　　Until I am replete
　　　　Yet there is always more

You are a wineglass -
　　Which never empties
　　　A crystal goblet -
　　　　That constantly nurtures
　　　　A purified chalice -
　　　　　Which endlessly receives
　　　　　　The treasure of our forever wine

# The Intimacy Of A Galaxy

Are you one of those trailblazing radicals
Who are adept at bowing down in reverence
As you navigate the rapturous gateway to ecstasy
That is accessed between a man and woman
Ravishingly entwined in authentic love?

Most can wrap their minds around
The sentimental intimacy of two lovers
The audacious self-revelation required
The sheer vulnerability demanded

Yet what about the primal mammalian patterns of intimacy
Among chimpanzees
Or a pack of dogs
Or a cluster of cats
That are emotionally entangled

What about the instinctive intimacy
Within a flock of geese
Parading across the sky in unison
Cooperating in an aerial formation
Of ascending grace?
Or the tango of two salamanders?
Or a ballet of earthworms?

What about the reflexive communion
Of stimulated bacteria?
Or very horny amoebas?
Or the ordered lattice structure
Of turned-on carbon atoms
Within a rough uncut diamond
Buried deep and silent
In the dense bedrock of the Earth?

If we could journey backwards
   Along time's evolutionary arrow
      Is there a distinct transmutation point
         Where the intimacy of carnal creatures adjourns
            And some unapproachable void begins?

Is a massive spiral galaxy able to be intimate
   With its nearest galactic neighbor?
      Or so different from a red-breasted robin
         As it feeds its newborn fledglings within the nest?

Can the swirling throng of a billion radial stars
   Let go of their individual separateness
      In order to merge - to mate with - to form a union
         With another luminous galaxy?

Does a galaxy have the faculty to be vulnerable
   To be able to trust enough
      To be willing to expose fears and limitations
         Without resistance or concern of being judged?

Could it honestly and brazenly
   Reveal its darker concealed aspects
      To its massive spiral neighbor?

Normally we don't allow ourselves
   To think about celestial galactic formations
      In this emotionally demonstrative manner

Yet if we did - if we could
   If we were radicals
      Isn't it possible for us to imagine
         That a gorgeously intelligent galactic goddess
            Could be completely and joyously awake and present
         As she's making amorous love
            During an intimate collision and ecstatic union
               With a nearby handsomely attractive galaxy?

Has the glimmering of timeless intimacy
   Continuously danced in existence
      Since the first flashes of the Big Bang?

Was intergalactic affection birthed into being
   With the initial explosive burst of The Great Radiance
      When the fervent *Souls*
         Of the first two sub-atomic particles amid the heavens
         Organically danced with a yearning
            To embrace their nuclear bodies as one?

Could it be that all this time
   This most natural intimate impulse
      Has been slowly morphing over the eons
         Through the perpetual revolution of cosmic ages
         With endless appearances
         Amidst myriad forms of lovers
         And as this eternal *Soul* feast
            Continues to unfold throughout the Universe
            Maybe we are just now
               Giving it a human flavor?

# It Only Takes One To Tango With God

Seductively I cradle my Tango partner
  In the web of my alluring arms
    Holding my Beloved pressed close to my heart
    Where I am entangled
      In the convergence of two universes
      Merging within the intimate play
     Of our endless radiance

A merging that's anchored within - and without
  That is one - and many
   Integrating the transcendent - with form

In the midst of this woven tapestry
  This intangible frolic of union
   We are danced as one existence
    Wherever we seem to find ourselves
     Whether spinning on the crest of mountains
      Or whirling within a curvaceous carved valley
     That lies between them

With enduring alignment
  We are danced over chiseled rocky ground
   Upon soft grassy meadows
    Where scented flowers thrive
    And ancient trees rot
     From the epic seasons of a previous age

In another flash we are danced
  Upon turbulent oceans
   Stirred by the horrific breath
    Of wild angry storms
     Then atop serene billowy clouds
      Passing the fragrant air of azure skies

And all the while
  Becoming cleverly skilled at the simple
    Yet not always easy steps
      Of this most vulnerable dance
        Through the resolve of choosing a higher orbit
          Heroic willingness to nudge the edges
            And courageously advancing the horizons
              One step after another
                Through all of *Love's* perplexing firestorms

For thousands of solar cycles
  Rehearsing the interlocking movements
    We refine our shifting routine
      Cultivate our natural communion

But no matter the uncertain terrain
  Our feet may traverse
    Within the sundry dance halls
      That we perpetually explore
        Our merger keeps us reaching further
          Through the next turning of the wheel
            Into ever lofty realms
              Of unbridled possibility

Yet during those fleeting moments
  In which the portal opens
    While we are divinely danced
      In the Grand Hall of Mirrors
        I every now and then
          Catch an ephemeral glimpse
            Of my cherished partner
              Noticing *the Beloved* I enfold so close
                Looks exactly like me
                  As if - all this time
                    I have been dancing with myself

# Winged Lovers

My grateful heart
  Shivers with ecstasy
    As my arms caress
      The contours of your aroused body

Feeling the flow of crimson blood
  Pulse through our rapturous veins
    I am draped in a lover's bliss
      Reaping the exalted revelation
        Of our sacred destiny
          Within passion's boundless journey
          As we humbly offer
            Our true essence to the stars

Starlight blazes in celestial triumph
  Each time we fervently pray
    To further awaken this love
      Each time we boldly surrender
      To the wild current
        Of love's unbridled stream

One more feather
  Is added to our wings
    That we may daringly soar higher
      Through the hallowed portal
        Of our next glorious awakening

# The Iceberg

I adore getting rapturously entranced
  In the star field of your luminescent eyes
    Amorously caressing
      The contours of our hallowed communion
        Feeling the erotic waves
        Of our oceanic love
          Wash over us for ephemeral moments
          That seem to transfigure into forever
        While we playfully taste
          The flavors of our ardent alliance
            Exploring the intimate caverns of our hearts
           And probing our passionate desires of …

(Oh! - No!!!!!!!!!! What's happening!!!!!!!!!!)

Suddenly - from an invisible portal into nowhere
  There abruptly sounds a torrential explosion
    The earth appears to rumble savagely under our feet
      Your inner volcano erupts
        Into a storm of fury
          Some iconic comment or notion I uttered
          Has sparked the notorious hidden trigger

With a few words our titanic outpouring of love
  Has hit an iceberg
    Oneness has come upon unexpected constriction
      Spaciousness has bumped into swift blockage
        Freedom has entered the prison of bondage
        And my untethered path with you
        Has met "the wall"

The pinnacle of an iceberg
  Always reveals its glimmering crest
    In the dazzling radiance of the Sun

Yet below the outward surface
    Of your pretty picture-perfect life
        That I meticulously painted upon your face
            With the brush of my embryonic illusions
                Lies a shadowy concealed beast from the unknown
                    And it's this mysterious stranger
                        That has twisted my angel
                            Into someone suspended far away
                                Within another world

Yet something primal and original
    Urges me to take a deep full breath
        Yes - a nourishing continuous connected breath
            The kind of centering breath
                That brings the departed back to life
                    A breath enabling me to perceive
                        Her iceberg is now delicately floating
                            On a still mirrored lake

And when I courageously
    Look straight into this mirror
        I notice the illusive iceberg
            Is actually my own reflection
                The frozen constriction is mine
                    The shadowy blockage is my construction
                        The dusty prison is of my own making
                            The crumbling wall is one I built long ago

So now I must choose
    Do I allow this massive recurring pattern within my life
        To hit the iceberg over and over again
            And sink me to the shadowy underbelly
                Of the Mighty Deep once more?
                    Or do I allow the sacredness of this mirror image
                        To be the hallowed gift
                            And holy messenger
                                That raises me up into the heavens?

# The Chessboard

The limitless supremacy of a thousand suns
Shimmers its perpetual radiance
Through a kaleidoscopic prism
Focusing its translucent rays into existence
Which we celebrate as reality
As if a celestial film projector
Was beaming each of us
Onto this vibrantly painted theater
Which we herald as the dance of life

There's only one *Light* flickering
As it emanates through life's cosmic projector
Yet it forms countless hues of characters on time's stage
Each an elaborately dressed actor
Performing their irreplaceable part
All the players nobly maneuvering
The next advantageous move
On the chessboard
The place where one might gather
How to love the entirety of life
A bit more fully

Some say our visionary friend
Who just masterfully played his final scene
Was executing his epic roles
On behalf of us all

For a blessed few he was a kind and caring father
As he crafted an exquisite life for his progeny
Helping them courageously jump from the nest
Feeling his colossal support and love-embrace
In whatever journey they embarked upon
Whoever they elected to become

He was king - warrior - magician - lover
　As an aspiring image to himself
　　And to the best of his ability
　　　For his regally adored queen
　　　　As he erected his castle walls - high and holy
　　　　　With a vision to protect her - from vile demons
　　　　　While in his heart - adorning her
　　　　　With the jewels of his fragile love

For many others on the chessboard
　He was friend - or foe - compatriot - or villain
　　High priest - or malevolent sorcerer - or both
　　　Acting out his roles as delegated to him
　　　　So those in his notorious pathway
　　　　　Could make a decisive move on the board
　　　　　To a higher rung of the ladder
　　　　　Ascending heaven's stairway
　　　　　Knowing the play's script
　　　　　Is surely about loving fully
　　　　　　Without limit - or reservation

Now he is somewhere
　Playing on a much bigger chessboard
　　One in which his wings touch realms of "no time"
　　　Within dimensions of "no space"
　　　　Where he shall summon forth his next strategic move
　　　　　Resolving when to make his next karmic leap
　　　　　Into the luminous beam of a thousand suns

We may one day again stand adjacent to him
　On some love-centered stage
　　Within the everlasting existence of our *Soul*
　　　Submerged in a sphere of amnesia
　　　　Performing our humble yet magnificent roles
　　　　　Over and over - until no more chess moves remain
　　　　　Except our destined checkmate
　　　　　Of loving one another - unconditionally

# Prayer To The Ancestors

A balmy sunrise wind
   Nimbly brushes against my cheek
      Gently swaying the desert's dry thorny branches
      While my head bows toward reverence

I silently invoke
   The hallowed bones of my ancestors
      As my prayer rides this delicate breeze
         Finding its way to those who sculpted me
         They that built the perennial tower
         From which I now leap

I celebrate these familial masons
   Clever artisans from past ages
      Keepers of earth wisdom
         Those still guiding my footsteps
            To the promised altar of freedom
               Whispering songs of my lifeblood
                  On behalf of everything that matters

The countless transcendent canticles
   Heralding Father - Heaven - Unmanifest
      Mother - Earth - all that is manifest

Mantras that speak of gentle kisses from grandmother
   Or the broad belly of grandfather
      Who forever smelled of musty wood
         When I nestled my arms round his core

Of their mothers and fathers prior to them
   As well as a host of the early ones
      Witnessing my tunneled memory travel inward
      Into a primal horizon of what once was

With eyes closed - mind at rest
   Attention turned toward an escalating silence
      I journey into my center
         Through a web of twisting pathways
            From spiral remembrances embedded
          Within each cell of my existence

I guardedly stroll the muddy corridors
   And prehistoric tree lines
      Where furry mammals and foreign creatures roam
         I survey an aboriginal matrix of trails
            Etched by the clans of hominids

These beasts - born within a flood of ferns
   The abrupt emergence of flowers
      And verdant vegetation of myriad hues
         All delivered into earthen form
            From a labyrinth of fish
               Spawned in the ocean's alchemy
            Of single-celled inventions

All of life's exhibitions
   Sculpted as a living ingredient
      Flavored within a primordial soup
         Of boiling lava rock
            That morphed into a hallowed banquet
          On a minor spinning globe
            A world flung from a nearby star

Certain stars have been forged
   To fling out their progeny
      For all emerges from radiance
         Everything that blinks and breathes
            Is a remnant of some exploding sun
               A solar forefather descending from the skies
                  In order to coalesce into spheres of light
               Into you - and me

I take a long urgent breath
  The sound of the desert wind stirs me
    Speaks to me
      Or is it - the whisper of the ancient ones
        And the rattle of bones

I know one day
  I will join this parade of ancestors
    Yet until I become a pearl
      On the necklace of this lineage
        The dazzling road sparkles before me
        My hands and my heart
          Listen for their songs
            The ones which inform me
              To fashion clay into wonder

Hence in every direction
  That the compass points me
    There beckons a vast field of stardust
      Waiting to be shaped
        For all that's given to imagine
          Is possibility

# VII

# ALTARS
# TO
# NATURE

# Call Of The Wild

Stillness slices through velvet air
As I sit on the wooded banks
Of this swollen emerald river
A billion footsteps
From the centers of chaos

The day is hushed and crisp
Enough to hear wings flailing
As red hawk darts across a tranquil sky
The nimble splashing of migrating ducks
Swimming as a regal parade
Diving for sustenance in the morning mist

In the crucible of this hallowed silence
Whispers the call-of-the-wild
A muted symphony of raven
The howl of wolf
A trumpeting of elk

No matter where I am
Whether the pristine sanctuary of nature's miracles
The four shielded walls of my abode
Or the crowded steel-girdered jungle
That cradles thousands of eyes
The call-of-the-wild beckons

It persistently tugs at me
Urges me to heed - to pay attention
Then entices me to indisputable safety
In the way a compass guides
An adventurer home
Or a beacon escorts
A lost ship to shore

Between every breath
  It sings a hymn to me
    When I close my eyes
      I watch it dance

Naturally the call-of-the-wild
  Does not serenade a solitary me
    For it echoes throughout every canyon
      Roars from every rooftop
        Rumbles at the heart of everything

It is the intrinsic call of nations
  Longing to dismantle their crumbling walls
    It is the incessant plea to prison guards
      Until at last their slaves and hostages are set free
        It is the frisky imaginations of children
          Pretending to pierce clouds like birds

It is the chameleon's alchemy
  Discovering more spectral ways to disguise
    The ancestral pine tree
      Learning to adapt to the mounting heat of winters

It is the ensuing collision of two galaxies
  Interweaving to fuse a new center point
    A universe in accord
      With the mystery of its one song

A ubiquitous call-of-the-wild
  Invites me to get naked again
    To peel away my lingering illusions
      To strip down to an essential core
        Where at this exalted shrine
          I am unsullied and innocent
            And from this golden throne
          I can declare and choose
            The audacity to create paradise

# Newborn Flowers

Newborn flowers arising from their verdant sheaths
   Exploding from stout yet fragile cocoons
      Drinking in the emergent light
         Then humbly offering celebration
            To the endless turning of seasons

The bones of ancestral beauty
   Found within the cradled infant
      The rebellious youth
         The blind lover
            And the one ripened by adventurous years
               Each forever blossoming becoming grander
            In the sweep of this interminable journey
                  Infinite petals all yearning for the wisdom of time
              To become ever fuller

What are the boundaries
   To this wellspring of *Being?*
      Are there any limits
         To how high nimble wings may ascend?
         Show me beyond illusion's edge
            Past the mirage of dreams
               Into the promise and shimmering
            Of a fresh uncharted world

There - over there
   Another audacious flower
      Keen to explore - eager to inquire
         To embrace an unfamiliar frontier of eternity's pledge
            Bursting with the prudence of silence
            Into a landscape of a million eyes
               Watching the natural world express
              Ever more of its effulgent self

# The Oak Tree

The burly ancestral legs of the oak tree
Have enabled this titan to stand there
Anchored to the stout bank of the river
With it's hungry fingerlike roots
Reaching downward for sustenance
Into a shrouded moist womb

Its verdant outstretched arms
Finger the dry parched air
That rarely dances
As half the spinning world melts
In the lingering hot summer

Yet the tall oak remains content
Peacefully gazing
Upon the tireless stream of flurry
The perpetual bustle of day and night

When the ritual colors of harvest flourish
The tree dawns its festive coat
Displayed in all four directions
The leafy landscape changes hues
Myriad creatures prepare for vicissitudes
As if a godly voice whispered them a secret

Within this fertile woodland circle
It seems those who choose not to listen
Cannot participate
In the unseen magic

Still - the tall oak stands in awe
Watching the constant movement
The perfect flow of the river's wild certainty

The icy heavens shower snow blankets
While sparse rays of sunbeams
Sparkle off jeweled droplets
Suspended like white diamonds
Amid the shimmering branches

Winter's wrathful storms
Have since blown away
The last crisp fragile leaf
That held on with a tiger's grip
Yet finally relaxed into free fall

And still - the tall oak sways
Embracing the raw course of the wind
Racing through its amenable arms

In time - like so many eons of yesterday
New patterns begin to take shape
New order yearns to blossom
New paradigms are eager to adorn

Once more the season of possibility makes its mark
As tiny seeds of a new horizon explode
Bursting from a native impulse
Of creation's everlasting dream

And as day gracefully passes into night
From wooded banks of an unrelenting river
Gently kissed by capricious winds
An oak tree simply grows
Merging more fully
With the tide of life's mystery
Rooted ever deeper
In an oceanic field of silence

# Flavors Of Paradox

I spoke - to the glistening chill of Winter
   The frozen hush of sparkling solace
      The cocooning spirit of suspended life in renewal
         And asked - if Winter was aware of the sultry heat of Summer
        The solar activation of a world made verdant again
         The burgeoning forth of living things in jubilation

Winter replied with a saddened heart
   Responding to rumored tales revealed by the Wind
      Of a sweltering season embracing radiance
      Of its kaleidoscopic lush vegetation
        Yet had no direct experience
           Of its nurturing climate - or its very existence

But I - have stood on the roof of the Moon
   And from that majestic tower of perspective
      Have looked down upon our shimmering globe
         Where both Winter's snow and Summer's rain
           Have plunged to the Earth during an identical moment
        Attesting to their symbiotic dance

A young child exploring life's twisted jungle pathways
   Who has not yet ascended
      To the crest of its steep mountain
        Cannot assemble the required comprehension
        In which God allows pain and suffering
        To canvas a brittle world
           Yet simultaneously God is Unconditional Love

Or that life's mutual timeline of past - present - and future
   Unfolds like a linear conveyor belt
      Yet nonetheless - concurrently
        There is only timeless eternity

A child does not yet know
   That he or she is a unique embroidering of existence
      That existence is one interconnected unity
         That unity constantly cycles through order and chaos
           Yet there is only perfection

Does not yet grasp that lifetimes are epic journeys
   From fear to Love
      But at the same time
         There is nowhere to go
           For only Love exists

I spoke - to an incomprehensibly small particle of light
   A distinct sunbolt of substantial luminance
      Physically hurtling through the firmament
         And asked - if this photonic particle knew of its twin sister
           The ubiquitous wave function of light
              The unseen quantum patterns
                 Etched on an immense sea of luminosity
                   Shaped from a pebble
                     Dropped by the Lord of Fire

The solar particle responded with a sigh
   Sadly recounting it knew not of any sister
      But only of its own solidity
         Its physical mass - its location in space
           Had never danced with - or ever encountered
              Its twin wave - its undulating field of light
                 And was unaware of its oscillating presence

But I - have stood at the podium
   Where the religion of quantum mechanics is sung
      A song whose stanzas herald a "Bigger Picture"
         Where the mystery and paradox of light
           Of both particle and wave
              Has grown accustomed to sleeping in the beds
                 Of our awakening minds

A great mystic cuts trails
　　Through the forest of darkness
　　　With razor-sharp questions
　　　　Allowing the Sun's rays
　　　　　To peer through the trees
　　　　　　Illuminating the perennial wisdom
　　　　　　　That he is a solitary expression of creation
　　　　　　And inconceivably
　　　　　　　Also *the Source of Creation*

That from incarnation after incarnation
　　She must experience every thought and feeling
　　　That appears and disappears in her world
　　　　And at the same time
　　　　　Knowing there is nothing to do
　　　　　There is only to be

A true mystic celebrates he is creation
　　And yet discovers he is also consciousness creating
　　　That she is a unique expression
　　　　Of an ever-evolving Universe
　　　　　And simultaneously
　　　　　She *is* the Universe

I then spoke - to the darkness of night
　　The black absence of quiescent radiance
　　　And asked - if it knew of the light of day
　　　　The full illumination
　　　　　Of an ever-blossoming world

The darkness answered sadly with a sigh
　　Revealing that the transient clouds
　　　Have told countless sagas of such a daytime light
　　　　Yet the darkness had no direct experience
　　　　　Of the light's actual ferocity

But I - have stood at the very center of the Universe
  Where I have watched
    The seeds of oak trees grow tall
      Tiny fledglings leap from their nests
        Where I have observed children
          Morph into mystics

The hallowed place where
  If I can remain at the banquet table
    And truly taste the feast of eternity
      Then I can look down on the face of GAIA
        See both the dark of night on one side of her belly
        The solar shine of day on her curved back
        And still savor the paradoxical claim
          That even though light and darkness
            Are needed to make this sacred body dance
          In another existence just as real
            Only *Light* exists

# Galactic Flower

He claims to be a simple man
Yet each time he reverently bows down
Humbly offering his bended knee to the Earth
To drink in the fragrance and splendor
Of another effulgent flower
He cannot but marvel
At the infinitely novel patterns
Of their intricate spinning contours
And dazzling spectral hues

His enormous presence
Standing over the blooms of these tiny petals
Appears as if he is a god
Gazing down into the vivid central hub
Of a tiny spiral galaxy
Intoxicated - mesmerized
Reveling with this resplendent creation
In his verdant garden Universe

For one brief instant
By his mere observation
He is *The Great Spirit*
Fashioning its pastel shades
Shaping its floral lines
With his laser-like attention

For a fleeting moment
He is *the Heavenly Father*
Eternally sustaining the essential spark
Of its very existence
By the manner in which
He affectionately looks
At his unfolding treasure

And he is *Shiva* eager to transform it
  After the final curtain has fallen
    At the end of an epic soliloquy
      Where this budding life form
        Has courageously proclaimed its willingness
          To wither and decay
            With the perpetual cadence of time

Whenever this simple man stands perfectly still
  Devouring the sublime silence
    In the kernel of a moment
      He is transmuted into a pair of magnifying eyes
        Peering deep into the translucent cells
          Of the flower's delicate fabric

Peering further down into the core of these petals
  He stares into its microscopic atoms
    With their orbiting electron moons
      Turning in an endless sea of spaciousness

We know that the infinitesimal small god of particle physics
  Is always watching electrons encircle protons
    While the gargantuan god of limitless cosmology
      Constantly observes moons rotating planets

Yet somewhere in the midpoint
  Of his long deep breath
    As he tastes the scent of possibility
      This simple man now sees his flower
        With notably different eyes
          Shifting from micro to macro
            From atom to global sphere
              For he now has become the lens
                That surveys the turning of day and night
              On a blue and white world
                Orbited by a single cratered moon
                  Traversing the silent halls of space

These dual terrestrial spheres - LUNA and GAIA
Tethered with numerous other worlds
Which also circumnavigate distant stars
Poetically arrange themselves
In immense star clusters
Which to this simple man
Appear to sculpt the contours
Of a great celestial flower petal

One individual petal floating in space
Within a fertile corner of the Cosmos
Coupled to a vast ring of countless petals
All merged in concert
Displayed around a massive central abyss
Which invisibly pulses at the heart
Of this colossal galactic flower

With the bliss of sheer rapture
He gazes fully
Into the rotary vortex
Of this dazzling petaled mystery

Maybe it requires a simple man
To practice being "a god in training"
To stand in the matrix of stillness
So as to one day enjoy
The fragrance of a galaxy

✳

✳ · ✳

✳

# VIII

# STORIES
## OF A MORE
## GLORIOUS
## WORLD

# The Healer

She easily maneuvered her sun-drenched sailboat
  Into the harbor of a small remote island
    Where one extinct mountainous volcano
      Loomed high above its white sandy beaches

She journeyed all this way to visit the famous one
  The one who lived at the edge of the volcano's rim
  The one who steered travelers
    To an affluence of miracles
      The one who people decreed
      Knew the holy secrets
        The one who was praised as "the healer"

After securing the boat she entered the nearby village
  The only hamlet throughout the entire island
  The place many expectant pilgrims came
    To inquire where the healer dwelled

The villagers pointed the traveler
  To a nearby mountain trail
    That ascended high into the thick green forest
    She climbed through the woodlands
      Until the path turned sparse and rocky
        Where she could look downward into a sweeping vista
      And gaze at the swirling ocean below
      That caressed its endless shores
    In every direction

After a few more arduous steps
  She saw a tiny quaint structure
    Positioned near the edge of the cinder cone
    An ornate temple built of rock and wood
    Painted with strokes of violet and red

An elderly astute-looking man
  Came out to greet her
    Dressed in a simple rugged robe and sandals
    And invited the journeyer to join him inside
      So the two marched through the timber entrance

Indoors the healer faced the pilgrim and immediately asked
  "Welcome - and why have you journeyed up this path?"
  With a bundle of despair in her heart she said
    "I have an affliction all throughout my body
      And I want to know - what I can do - to be healed"

The healer smiled compassionately - and declared
  "I am an instrument of infinite miracles
    I am the keeper of nature's secrets
    If you want to heal your affliction
      You must go to the village below
        Purchase a purple amethyst and cobalt quartz
        Take the two stones to your bedside
        Place one on each side of your bed
        Then surrender into sleep"

The woman joyously thanked the healer
  Ran immediately down the highland trail
    Strolled into the village store
    Purchased the two exotic stones
      Found a charming inn nearby for the night
      Placed the stones on each side of her bed
      And fell into a dreamy sleep

The next morning
  She excitedly jumped out of her night's cradle
    Dashed over to the mirror
    To examine her body
      And found that her right arm
      Was completely healed
        Yet the rest of her body remained afflicted

Mired with turmoil the traveler scurried up the ascending trail
To again arrive at the healer's temple
She found him meditating in the garden
The healer opened his eyes and spoke softly
"Welcome - and why have you journeyed up this path?"
The afflicted one proclaimed with sadness
"My body is still plagued with this affliction
Except for my right arm - which is restored
What can I do - to be healed?"

The healer again smiled compassionately - and declared
"I am an instrument of infinite miracles
I am the keeper of nature's secrets
If you want to heal your affliction
You must go to the village below
Purchase the elixir of an orchid flower
Ingest it under the light of the full moon
Then go to sleep"

With new hope the woman left in gratitude
Descended into the now familiar village
Bought a vial of the special elixir
Waited until the moon rose above the horizon
Swallowed its promise of recovery
Then relaxed into bed for a deep slumber

At dawn she awoke to a wild anticipation
Darted toward the mirror to inspect
And found her left leg had joined the right arm
In a celebration of wholeness and wellbeing
Yet the rest of her body
Remained challenged from the enduring infirmity

The traveler immediately returned to the mountain temple
Where the healer was chanting a song of devotion
When he saw her - he stopped singing and said
"Welcome - and why have you journeyed up this path?"

The afflicted one screamed with frustration
  "Parts of me are still tormented
    What can I do - to be healed?"

The healer once again smiled caringly - and declared
  "I am an instrument of infinite miracles
    I am the keeper of nature's secrets
      If you want to heal your affliction
        You must take this holy scroll
          And recite this restorative declaration 108 times
            While you're standing with your feet
              In the water of gentle ocean waves at sunset
                Then immediately go to bed"

With promise again in her heart she left the temple
  After thanking the healer for the scroll
    Waited patiently all day until sunset
      Took off her shoes and waded into the waves
        Recited the healing statement 108 times
          Then returned to her room and dropped into sleep

In the morning she went to the mirror
  Only to find her chest had joined the right arm and left leg
    Yet the remainder of her aching body
      Was still staggering from the uncomfortable affliction

With a radical mixture of anger and rising detachment
  She slowly made her way up the trail to the healer's temple
    And found the healer waiting at the door
      With great empathy in his eyes he repeated
        "Welcome - and why have you journeyed up this path?"

There was a long yielding pause
  And then the woman who had journeyed
    So far across time and space to find renewal
      Whispered from a truly surrendered heart
        "Who must I be - to become - truly healed?"

Hearing this the healer relaxed into a profound serenity
   Then with a prudent smile spoke softly
     "Please enter my dear one"
      After a commanding silence he said
       "So - I now feel - your sincerest intention"

"If you had asked me that initially I would have told you
   To place all your attention
     On the birds as they sing
      In the verdant trees of the forest
       And let their nurturing songs
        Saturate every cell of your body
         With a rapturous joy that brings enchanted harmony

I would have told you
   To focus all your awareness
     On the exquisite beauty of this orchid
      So you may drink in the splendor of its patterns
       Its wild intricacies - its radical wonders
      And let it bathe you with a holiness
     That vibrates within all things

I would have told you
   To close your eyes and open your heart
     As you picture within you the ones you love
      So you may give *the Infinite Love* that you are
       To each and every one of them
        For that *Sacred Love* circles back to you
       To pulsate your very being
        With the vibrant fullness of eternity

I would have told you
   To look into this mirror
     So you may celebrate the perfection of it all
      And proclaim in glory's ecstasy
       That everything that's happening in and through you
      Is a profound gift of life

For the magnificent ocean of boundless unity
    That we bravely sail each day
        Is constantly sending out its ever-transforming waves
            The vast waves of experience we must learn to ride
                Each one in unconditional gratitude

Therefore - for each pilgrim who comes to me
    And chooses to ride this sublime wave
        The one who can truly embrace the song of the birds
            Who can truly see the exalted beauty of the orchid
                Who can truly open to the mighty love between loved ones
                And who can truly celebrate the mirror of the *Self*
                    Then that journeyer becomes a person
                        Who is - and who has always been - truly healed"

After an infinite moment of communion
    The traveler began to notice
        A torrential wind began to build in every direction
            Violently shaking the ground under her feet
            And fiercely rattling the temple
                The wind and its haunting sound grew massively potent
                Until the entire sanctuary
                    Started to crumble all around her

An immensely vigorous cyclone
    Utterly destroyed the temple
        And her surrounding world
            Was in absolute chaos

Yet the journeyer sat within a glorious peace
    Sanctified within the silent center of the tempest
        Where she heard the singing
            And saw the beauty
                And felt the love
                And celebrated the *Self*
                And honored the healer
                  As she gave thanks for her perfect body

# The Prospector's Trophy

He was renowned as a seasoned prospector
Who devoted his enterprising life
Combing creation for arcane treasures
Attempting to reveal
What others had not yet uncovered
Myriad wonders buried untold
In a shrouded belly of the Earth

So once again he searched
Meandering through subterranean caverns
Inspecting lengthy obscure tunnels
For the perfect flawless diamond
The one ever eluding him
His supreme imminent prize

Suddenly the fabric of his world trembled
For on this day witnessed his quest fulfilled
Catching a glimpse of scant sparkles
Behind a skeletal layer of a timeless wall
The surprise glistening of a mammoth gem

Upon scrubbing away surrounding debris
He carefully elevated his find
Seizing it firmly in both hands
As if caressing a translucent trophy
Or a crystalline chalice
Yet still rough - jagged - uncut
Which demanded the polishing skills
His expertise had acquired

Eagerly he carted the luminous diamond to his haven
Where he stowed his menagerie of mining gear
And positioned the cherished jewel
On a well-lit wooden table

Fervently he commandeered a polishing drill
  Began to artfully shape the gemstone
    Yet each time he struggled to sculpt his treasure
      He could not transform its outline
        Or alter its appearance in any way

In torment he gripped a second tool
  And again set out to polish
    Yet the cherished rock would not change
      Then with a third instrument
        But once more he could not modify it

After a long arduous sigh of surrender
  He sensed the advent of a warm hint of gratitude
    For the fruitful adventure he occupied
      The victorious explorations of the cryptic cavern
        The fortune to uncover this enormous gift

Instantly one facet of the diamond
  Transmuted from rough and uncut
    To smooth and perfectly polished
      As if some magician's spell had pierced the room
        Invisibly sculpting his prize
          With an enchanted command

Astonished - he was dazed with more grateful elation
  That one facet of his gem was impeccably fashioned
    Then again before his eyes - a second facet altered
      From its coarse jagged profile
        To a finely polished surface

Abruptly from habitual bewilderment - he began to complain
  That his trusted polishing tools did not always succeed
    In shaping the staggering treasure which lay before him
      And as he sought to polish another facet
        The diamond once again refused to shift
          Standing anchored in frozen silence

After a few deep relaxing breaths
His mind again reverted to a grateful air
That at least two glistening facets
Were superbly honed into precision
Then astoundingly - a third facet formed

Somehow in a spontaneous flare
He conjured gratitude for all his friends
And a fourth facet arose
He sensed appreciation for his health
A fifth facet took shape
Then thankful for the glorious day
Another facet came into being
Grateful for providence of the moment
An additional facet
He finally gave thanks
For every feature in his life
And all the diamond's facets
Formed with seamless alchemy

There in front of him within the dazzling light
Laid the most perfectly sculpted diamond
This prospector eyes had ever beheld

The first thought to tempt his mind
Was to sell his immaculate gemstone
And tap his massive abundance
To fulfill every worldly desire
He aspired to ensnare

So he hurried toward the worktable
To gather up the colossal diamond
That he might ferry it to market
But as he tried to lift it
The gem had transformed into a thousand tons
And with all his strength
It would not budge

After much crucial silence a benign thought arose
   Instead he would place the diamond in a museum
      Where it could be displayed
         Within a gloriously supreme setting
           Employing the most dynamic lighting
         To enhance its radiance
           For people to enjoy
              Elevating the spirits of many

With this virtuous notion he reached to lift the jewel
   Yet even though it was still quite heavy
      He could now grip it in his hands
         And manage to carry it away

But before he maneuvered a step
   He was compelled to gaze deeply
      Into the diamond's alluring core
         As every one of its polished facets
           Became a sheer reflecting mirror
              In which he witnessed his true perfect self
           His own magnificence
           His radiant holiness
              His oneness with the ultimacy of life
           His sublime divinity

When his exalted vision faded
   He was absolutely certain
      He must now share his gem
         With everyone he knew
           That they might also peer into its center
              To experience their most sacred splendor
           Their true radiant selves

As the pristine moment of this noble thought
   Softly embraced his heart
      The perfect diamond he held in his hands
         Became lighter than a feather

# A Journey Into The Light Of *Being* And *Becoming*

She relaxed completely into the quantum portal
  The hallowed threshold to the precious moment
    Gathered a handful of satisfying breaths
      Then softly soared into imperceptible spaciousness
        Feeling serene and sublimely tranquil
          So utterly at ease
            She effortlessly began to float upward
              Spontaneously ascending to the crown of the room

As her eyes glanced downward
  She caught sight of her physical body still lying below
    Where it was initially laid
      Yet *the Radiant Essence of her Being* was floating above
        Gazing down at her resting form
          Enjoying a deified sense of absolute freedom

Then - as an orb of dazzling light
  Her numinous *Essence* towered higher into the air
    Passed through the dense fabric of the ceiling
      Entering the gateway of a long spiraling tunnel
        Comprised from a million fragments
          Of countless vivid luminosities
            That she began to journey through
              Without any attempt on her part

She was transported through a shimmering passage
  Noticing far away in the distance
    A commanding resplendent *Light*
      And as she advanced toward this alluring *Brilliance*
        Found herself gifted with a radical understanding
          Of the superior nature within all existence
            Feeling ever more loved
              As she approached its *Boundless Illumination*

At last the tunnel ended
  Where she halted her advance
    Pausing before this ecstatic *Light*
      Being bathed in an overwhelming aura
        An elated communion
          With the grandest *Unconditional Love*
            She had ever embraced
          A *Love* so euphoric
            So compassionate
            So perfect
                She yearned to remain forever

Immersed in this benevolent *Field of Love*
  She felt showered within sublime peace
    As nurturing waves of a true happiness abounded
      Her adventure heralded a sense of authentic joy
        In the endless helix of a most sacred harmony

She began to melt into its omniscient *Light*
  To merge with its luminous *Centerpoint*
    To be one with this *Limitless Power*
      Cloaked in the realization
        That she was home
          Where she instantly fathomed
            The supreme purpose
              For everything in the Universe
                For she was
                  Has always been
                    And will ever be - *this Light*

She had leaped
  Into an *Unbounded Ocean of Being*
    Where there was nothing to do
      Except to be
        *The Light of Absolute Love*

- - - - - - - - - - - - - - - - - - - - - - - - - - - - - - - - - - - - -

Following a brief rapture into grace
She then heard the faintest sound
From a place she knew so well
The clarion call from a gentle heartbeat
The heartbeat of *Becoming*
Beckoning her to pursue its pulse

She welcomed its soothing rhythm
Envisioning herself drifting warmly
Within the womb of her mother
And with a mighty burst of supremacy
Was thrust through the birth canal
Into a vibrant world of possibility
To join an expansive field of limitless choices

She pictured every one of her life episodes unfurl before her
As if she hovered inside a three-dimensional theater
Reliving everything she ever experienced
Every choice she ever made
Every breath she ever breathed
During the transient fullness of her life

Only this time each event became a fleeting instant
Each emotion was felt as if happening in the present
She intuited the sentiments
Embraced the thoughts
Of every person involved
In her life's myriad adventures
Following each success - each failure
Every pain - every joy

Then she received a prescient glimpse
Into an alternative storyline for her life
Of other more awakened choices
She might have made that if chosen
Could have augmented the creation
Of an even more glorious world

In an incomparable flash of transcendence
She relived all the experiences and emotions
During the full span of her life
From her first breath to the current moment
With awareness of all she had learned
Amidst a bountiful perspective of her existence
Then was told to let go of every luxuriant memory
So she could once again return
To the pure translucent diamond she has always been

As her "life review" and every remembrance was gloriously set free
The new luminescent *Radiance* that she became
Was encircled by a host of majestic *Light Beings*
Her personal teachers and guides
The avatars and angels who helped her progress
Along her inner and outer *journey of awakening*

In the revered presence of these *Beings of Light*
She felt cradled in complete safety and protection
Enfolded in arms of the most nurturing love
Fully empowered
To do all the magnificent things
And give the unique gifts to the world
She was destined to offer

Then without a single word - all of these *Beings*
Communicated with her as one silent voice
Informing her - this is the moment she was to return
To the world of *Becoming*
To the realm of her physical body

And so once again she entered the long tunnel
Descending toward the world of form
She began to hear an ethereal song
Sung by the voices of paradise
That seemed to beckon
From every corner of existence

Slowly she journeyed down the luminous passage
  Immersed in this celestial music
    Filling her with a prophetic knowing
      She was about to enter
        A phenomenal world of time
          Yet simultaneously she recognized
            There is only the never-ending peace
              Of timeless eternity

Her *Soul* was granted a gift of understanding
  That she had an important destiny
    To fulfill with her physical body
      Yet in the same instant
        She understood
          There is nothing to do
            There is only to be - *the Light*

The exalted melody surrounded her
  With a profound knowing
    That the outer world of form
      Is an awakening quest
        Guiding her from fear to *Love*
          Yet she also realized
            Only *Love* exists

The heavenly incantation infused in her a sublime wisdom
  That she would soon enter a reality
    In which she was an individual expression of the Universe
      Yet still she was fully aware
        She *is* the Universe

She was about to place her feet
  Into a world of experience
    In which life journeys through constant cycles
      Of order and chaos
        Yet at the same time she knew with certainty
          There is only unfolding perfection

The ecstatic music filled her
   With a spacious awareness
     She was about to enter
       A world of time and space
         Where darkness and suffering
           Exist amid the light
             Yet simultaneously she recognized
             Everything is God
               *The Absolute Light of Eternal Unbounded Love*

Then as she reached the tunnel's end
   She watched herself effortlessly glide
     Right through a dimensionless barrier
       And found once again
         She was floating at the top of the room
           Where below her physical body rested

She looked down at her mortal outline
   Feeling such gratitude for the vessel she'd been given
     Embracing complete surrender
       Concerning the coming journey
         She was about to embark upon
           Accepting her earthly mission with fervor
           Realizing she was undeniably one
             With all she was about to experience

And so she descended from the crest of the room
   Drifting down toward her waiting body
     Her *Radiant Essence* once again
       Gently merged with her physical form
         As she opened her eyes with elation
           Eager to contribute her creative gifts and talents
           To a world of infinite possibilities
             To be in service to *Life*
               In ways that only she could serve
             To give to others
               In ways that only she could give

# Physics Of The *Soul*

Once long ago upon the Earth there lived only 1000 original humans
   With each human body inhabiting one eternal *Soul*
      As time passed and all of these initial humans died
         There were 1000 *Souls* gracefully existing in the afterlife

Eventually these 1000 *Souls* were told to return to the Earth plane
   So as to become the second generation of humans in 1200 new bodies
      Yet now there would be 200 more bodies than *Souls* within the world
         Since in the beginning there prevailed only 1000 human *Souls*

So several of the original *Souls*
   Decided to subdivide their true essential nature
      In order that their one distinct solitary *Soul*
         Could now become two

Just like when a human embryo within the mother's womb
   Is fertilized by the male seed
      Then the initial single cell within the embryo
         Is mystifyingly split - and wondrously becomes two

Not all of the original 1000 *Souls* were required - or able - to divide
   Since only 200 additional human bodies
      Were brought into carnal expression
         From the second generation of 1200 births

So a cosmic agreement was rendered
   That those initial *Souls* who had lived on Earth
      And learned to experience a rich lifetime
         Of inner growth and expanded development
            Would be the chosen few
               Who would have the celestial sanction
                  Of being impregnated by *the Father of Life*
                  And transcendently divide into two *Souls*

The *Souls* whose lifetimes on Earth
  Who did not use their precious moments
    To learn what really matters
      Or find ways to benefit others
        Would remain solitary the way they were
        And not divide in two

These *Souls* who were lazy and stagnated
  Wasting their precious life
    Who did not improve or progress
      Found themselves back
        At the very beginning again
          All alone in one human body
            To try once more
              This was called Hell

Those *Souls* who chose to grow and develop
  Who learned to give and serve one another
    Were bestowed with the celestial blessing
      Of splitting into two *Souls*

And the two divided *Souls* were each assigned
  New youthful incarnations on Earth
    In two distinct bodies of male and female
      Dual beloveds destined to find one another
        To continue their mutual advancement
          Into realms of limitless possibility
            And the prospect for sacred rapture
            This was called Heaven

# Paradise Is Only A Breath Away

Strolling into the dimly lit theater
  Carrying his staunch curiosity
    He swiftly acquired a seat midway
      Awarding him a paramount view
        To witness the film's staggeringly provocative images
        His hunger satiated with half a bag of popcorn

A most unparalleled motion picture
  Began to unfurl its mesmerizing saga
    An outrageously novel movie
      In which he found that each breath he took
        Was the creative genesis at the core of its epic tale

Every time he drew a hefty inhale into his center
  He breathed in a few possibilities
    Of what the film's outward existence might express
      Each exotic cerebral image
        Crossing the private screen of his mind
          Allowed another intimate prospect of creation
            Until finally he commanded a corresponding exhale
              Projecting an explosive emergence of a fiery Big Bang
            A vast ubiquitous Universe
              Arriving on the cinema's screen
                Breathing out his mammoth imaginings
              As a colossal structure of massive energy
              Appearing into form one moment
                Somehow gone with his next breath

He then inhaled an utterly new conception
  Another distinctive reality
    Conjuring vivid notions of ephemeral waves of energy
      And quantum particles of luminosity
        One buoyant flavor of his myriad possible universes

His exhale shaped his next outward formation
   Launching a host of colliding galaxies
      Exploding stars
         And molten volcanic planets
            That cooled into seasoned landscapes
               A throng of rocks and jewels and grit
                  All ultimately disappearing from view
                    Into a blackish gulf of emptiness

He again inhaled probability
   His newest vision of perceptual invention
      A whimsical prophecy
         Of multifarious creatures
            While his exhale sculpted upon the screen
               An endless menagerie of curvaceous organisms
                  Swimming in oceans of articulate storylines
                  Crawling upon the sands of history
                  Carnivores devouring one another
                  With an intrinsic yearning
                    To persevere the raging storms
                    To survive another tomorrow
                  Until his latest imaginings
                      Dissolved into nothingness once more

He took another copious inhale
   Envisioning a further revelation
      Of fledgling hominids
         Reaching for advanced intelligence
            While his vigorous exhale
               Unveiled a domain of warring tribes
               Battling ideologies
             Political absurdities
               Belligerent religious doctrines
                  And a few small islands of awakened sanity
               Until this latest universe
                  Gradually melted with his receding breath
                  Into the abyss of a translucent void

He noticed himself pausing for a moment
To look away from the screen
To briefly shift in his seat
To thoroughly gaze
At a sliver of silence
Wrapped in successive spheres
Of fresh perspective
Then enjoyed a handful of popcorn
While at once recognizing
Where this movie was headed

So he boldly welcomed
The film's existential challenge
Watching himself take a last daring inhale
One more time
Breathing deep from his core
Maximum and exceedingly full
Yet from a sovereign hallowed place
An estate where he had never experienced
Such exalted superior air

With a transcendent inhalation
That surfaced from a higher orbit of his mind
As well as his sublime luminous heart
He envisioned still
Another promising universe

This time an uncommon but longstanding reality
A vast community of radical awakening
A global tribe of compassionate living
In ecstatic union
With the natural world
As he audaciously exhaled
Into unmistakable form
The most simple and obvious
Yet stunningly glorious paradise

# IX

# GATEWAYS
## TO AN INVISIBLE
## RAINBOW

# We Begin Again

And so - we begin again
   We begin once more
      As we have done so many times before

We ignite a blaze of passion
   Pulsing within our marrow
      We beat our drums
         And shake our rattles
            We sing our creation songs
            Waiting patiently
               On the edge of our lips

We dance wildly to an ageless rhythm
   To the original heartbeat of the world
      To an unrelenting mantra calling for freedom

We have done all this before
   Yet we've been summoned once again
      To journey farther within *The Great Circle*
         To beat another drum
            To chant another song
            To dream another dance
               To touch the next horizon
                  Of all that's perfect within the spiral mystery

Oh yes - we've adventured here before
   And still our hearts recognize
      There is nowhere to go
         There is nothing to do
            Yet life beckons us to sail on
            To realize our sacred destiny
            And so - we begin again
               And again - and again

# Fork In The Road

Billions of us are carried by a blue and white pearl
As we ride its shimmering roller coaster through space
So many motley shapes - sizes - colors - faces
Yet we all ultimately traverse identical journeys
Migrating toward a targeted destination
Seeking equivalent essential nourishment
At the global banquet table

Some call our human expedition "the road of life"
Others label it "the agony and the ecstasy"
"The daily grind"
"The stairway to heaven"
"The epic human odyssey"
"The hallowed voyage of one's evolution"
"The immortal blossoming of the *Soul*"

However we position our saga in some neat little box
It's simply true that as we navigate the journey
Our excursion meanders through surprise twists and turns
Myriad mysterious crossroads along the way

Or another way to think about it
Is that with every step upon our path
There is a fork in the road
Two tracks before us
Which we must deliberately select
To go either right - or left
This way - or that way
Take the high road - or the low road
The path to heaven
Or the path towards hell
The way of the enlightened
Or the way of the yet-to-be-enlightened

One path is like becoming a maple leaf
  Floating effortlessly downstream
    Upon the surface of a surging river
      Utterly surrendered to the unknown adventure
     Of the water's relentless current

The other is like opting to sit
  In a large metal cauldron
    Churning with searing water
     Brewing hotter and hotter
      Placed over a sizzling bonfire
       And feeling ever more constricted by the second

Each of the many billions of us
  Come to this fork a thousand times a day
    Strolling this way or that
     Discovering heaven or hell
      Only we tend to contrive
       That certain momentary choices
        Are more important than others
         Some much bigger in economy or intensity
        Others more prominent and obvious

Yet from that grand deified perspective
  Where life simply is as it is
    Does it really matter which fork in the road
     We decide upon?
      For this mystic vantage decrees
       We're eventually going to arrive
      At our date with destiny either way

Could the fullness of existence
  Be so cleverly designed
    For ever-increasing flowering?
     Could the entire Cosmos
      Be intentionally fashioned
       For ever-grander unpacking of our glory?

When at last we attain
   The wild and free viewpoint of the eagle
      Could there be only one
         True direction to explore?

This Universe seems to contain
   An infinite amount of time
      To fulfill its every heart's desire
         Yet we - in this one particular lifetime
            Seem to possess
               A brief and limited span of moments
             To fulfill our *Soul's* longing
                  During this magnificent incarnation

In every blessed moment
   Perfection is blooming
      We can always pick either fork
         For we're ultimately destined
            To appear at heaven's gate one day
         No matter what we do

Yet when we daringly choose
   To embark the high road
      I bet the roller coaster ride
         Is going to be a lot more fun

❋

❋　·　❋

❋

# Halfway To An Infinite Forever

One day in some nearby tomorrow
I would enjoy being an astronaut
On a lofty planetary orbit
Cruising around our terrestrial home
At dizzying speeds
Peering through
The spacecraft's thick glass window
To celebrate our blue and white orb
As it hurtles through a field of stars

It would be my exalted throne
Where I watch the birth
Of awareness-seeking life forms
Swimming within its tides and eddies
Who reach for that same field of stars
A regal place to imagine the possible
To envision the future track
Where this spinning pearl
Might feasibly be headed
Thrust downstream
By a current of endless promise

For our Beloved Earth
Has been slowly sculpting its contours
Patiently shaping its inhabitants
For over four billion years

Yet in another mere four billion
Our central Sun
Will burn out into oblivion
Its fiery splendor will vanish
Our solar system will succumb
To an eclipsed silence

Miraculously we have made it
    Halfway to the finale
        Midway to the closing target date
            Within our tiny corner of the Cosmos

A time when medial stars of other solar systems
    Which dot the Milky Way
        Will also be ablaze
            Curdling to ashes
                When every neighboring galaxy
                    Will be propelled faraway from sight
                        From the gaze of our most capable telescopes
                            When the once star-lit Universe
                            Will sway into darkness

Yet energy cannot be destroyed
    Only ceaselessly transformed
        Transmuted into perpetual renewal
            Along an infinite spiral ever grander

All surface forms of life
    Have fathomed how to ingest nourishment
        From a passing sunbeam
            Through the conquest of food
                The simplicity of breath
                    Through skin's absorption of light

Yet before our dawning solar giant
    Incinerates its precious fuel
        During our future revolutions
            We will covet more creative ways
                To consume the Sun's illuminations
                    Inwardly adapting our physical forms
                        To bring to bear future innovations
                            Eventually arising as non-physical beings
                                Who have steadily morphed
                                    Into the endowment of luminous energy

Looking down from an orbiting spacecraft
I can clearly follow our human trajectory
Observing how far we've traversed
On our long arduous quest
Toward more noble awakening

A collective act that could possibly linger
For four billion more
During which we might venture outward
To neighboring stars
Meeting with other galactic consorts
Procreating with the radiant hosts
Of faraway water-laden planets
Who also occupy
This ever-shrinking cluster of suns

Making love within the arms
Of a mystically surrendered heart
Offering the kiss
Of ever loftier awareness
Is the sublime transcendent music
That intertwines us as a singularity

For as shimmering beings from a million stars
All dancing in supernal harmony
Built with streams of resplendent power
And merging at the central hub of this galaxy
We must - in time - surely coalesce
As one universal luminosity

Then as the last stars
Are finally extinguished
One by one throughout an infinite forever
In the darkened silence of our Cosmos
It will be time to say once again
United as one voice
"Let there be Light"

# The Awakening Of A God-Hunter

At the completion of a long turbulent sleep
Following interminable blinded walks
Through the ephemeral darkness
After swimming against a never-ending current
A river of recurring illusory dreams and nightmares
Laid out like an invisible ribbon
Interwoven in the fleshy fabric
Of her star-reaching life
She woke up
Listening to the reverberations
Of the laser-like question
"Who am I?"
Echoing across her heart

Every tiny molecule
Of her *Soul's* stardust
Proclaimed in its own voice
All roaring in concert
Booming together
With the raw primal explosion
Of a birthing universe
As she heard herself
Sing out in triumph

"I am a god-hunter
Sculpting god into form
Humbly serving
The many faces of god
Ever mindful
I am a facet
Of a god-diamond
Who always gazes
Into the mirror of god"

Then she commanded
  "Let there be Light
    And the blossoming
      Of a most magnificent day
        And a more glorious world"

But first
  It was time for breakfast

Railroad Trestle in Telluride, CO

# Monument Of Time

Here before me - stands a monument of time
  A broken withered railroad trestle
    Silent - yet whispering its ageless story
      An ancestral bridge from one earthen shore to another
        Where blazing iron horses
          Once slithered through wilderness air
            Fording oceans of untamed frontiers

Now the cracked timbers within this monolith
  Sag and creak on its once mighty skeleton
    Like the deformed back of a wrinkled man
      After a lifetime of burden
        No crossings have touched its charred spine
          In what seems a thousand moons
            And the hammers of weather
              Threaten to chisel its beams into splinters

Yet a patient miracle has waited in the wings
  Eager to emerge from behind veiled corners
    For somewhere in the muddled dome of institution
      The hope of humanity lunged out
        To fervently renew this treasure of time

With enough political will
  Enough communal resources
    Enough societal courage
      One can now detect echoing within the ravine
        The renovating drone from the promise of healing

Here before me - I witness the brawny business of men
  Strengthening olden legs of the wooden beast
    Mending the wounds of its regal history
      Bandaging its crumbling pillars

Nobly restoring its honor and dignity
   So that you and I may reach into its future
     May celebrate the majesty
      Of its architectural power

Here within me - I have regularly inspected
   The collapsing of my own timbers
     The gradual decay
      Within the once colossal beams
     Of my own cherished trestle
      For time and the friends of time
       Have chipped away at its foundation

Yet eyes are created to gaze at the possible
   Hearts beat that they may touch new horizons
     Bridges of thought are forever built
      To cross from ignorance to wisdom
      From demon to deity

Through the majesty of grace one can find within
   Enough will to demonstrate intention
     Enough resourcefulness to renovate choice
     Enough courage to transform belief

Here within me - also stands a monument of time
   Intention built upon choice and belief
     The promise of metamorphosis
     The enduring hope of a butterfly

✳

✳ · ✳

✳

# Spectrum Of Order And Chaos

There are moments when I'm temporarily captured
Within a sphere of unexpected elation
Seized by a fleeting rapture of epiphany
Where the acquiescent eyes of my heart
Are awarded the exultation of a prime awareness
The lucidity of sacred paradox
Which always invigorates me
Masquerading this time
As an invisible rainbow

Yet I am not always able to remain there
Pulled away during virtual episodes of divide
When my eyes observe a mere fragment
Of the full multicolored spectrum
An incomplete subplot
A partial narrative

A storyline enabling me to only focus on pristine order
Creation's invention of exquisite symmetry
Embodied by a few isolated violets and blues
A fractional slice of reality's broad continuum
Which I sometimes enjoy as an azure sky
Or a sapphire dawn dripping down upon my crown
As it shrouds me in its indigo cocoon
Warm and snug like a royal silken robe

Oh - what vast construction
Of meticulous celestial precision
The one wing of life's kaleidoscopic spectrum
Shaping intelligent pattern and organic design
Heralding rigorous cosmic clockwork
Proclaiming a natural self-regulating mathematics
That dances through every minimal speck
Of dust and fire - particle and wave

This lavender flower
   Emerging from that visionary seed
     This magenta creature
       In response to that pioneering strategy
      This amethyst lifetime
        Written from that superior script

Yet I am also lured away from this welcome rapture
   During those conflicting times of my journey
     When I'm inadvertently caught
       By an opposite wing of the spectral scale
      When these bewildered eyes
        Look not upon life's ordered realm of violets and blues
        But on a wild random creation

When for a flock of moments
   I'm only able to remember unruly terrestrial reds
    And chaotic shades of orange
      Where it feels like the blood of life's breath
      Appears and then disappears
       Through my balmy veins
        As it pulses to a much different song
         Or sometimes it seems like a saffron monk
        Praying within a crimson labyrinth
          While strolling through a baffling language door
        To a foreign land

Within these discordant hues of probability
   My solitary ship meanders
    Amid a potentially haphazard sea
     There are no predictable harbors
       For me to anchor the accidental chains of reason
       Destinations are slippery with chance
        For they may lead me to Eden
        Or lay me down in a field of Eternity
         Or without warning leave me stranded
         Within a scarlet inferno of hell

How wondrous!
　How deliciously magical!
　　Show me the gods who have conjured up
　　　This constant changing of the guard
　　　　These altering colors of enterprise

Who in one moment
　Melt the ores of chaos
　　So it all may vanish
　　　In their fiery galactic furnace
　　　And in another
　　　　Forge swords of scrupulous order
　　　　　That we might ever so briefly
　　　　　　Fight off a dread fear of the unknown

Oh alas! What sweet mystery!
　Could the very fabric of my life
　　Be so whimsically out of control
　　　Lost between a motley dance
　　　Of order and chaos
　　　　Like a crisp fragile autumn leaf
　　　　Flung from a mother oak
　　　　　By the tumultuous winds of uncertainty
　　　　　And thrust into the holes
　　　　　　Of unanswered questions?

What colorful parallel roads do I traverse
　That take me across this mutable rainbow
　　Sometimes to eternity
　　　And sometimes to my mortal carnal flesh?

Does it beckon me to endlessly create
　Every majestic vision within my heart
　　With the knowing I must relinquish
　　　Each exquisite masterpiece
　　　At every breath?

Yet within all fleeting moments of order - or chaos
That I confront upon this illusive binary path
Whichever branch of the fork I settle upon
As these awakening eyes
Navigate this spectral arc of promise
The voice of perpetual silence
Forever whispers upon my ear
A simple invitation
That my willing heart's response
Be ever the same

Sing - the *Soul's* canticle
In service to the Tree of Life
Bend - like a supple willow
When the wind is raging
Merge - with the flowing current of a wild river
Destined to be reunited
With the ubiquitous ocean that awaits

# Questions

Gazing skyward within a dome of diamonds
  In midnight silence
    A colossal unfathomable Universe
      Enveloping billions of galaxies
        A plethora of stars peppering every one
        Possibly a million worlds
          Reminiscent of this blue pearl
        Where mortal feet
          Nestle hallowed ground

Yet as far as can now be established
  Humans reign as the only creatures
    In any corner of the Cosmos - who question

Do I need a better toothbrush?
  Should I buy a thinner TV?
    Do I need to lose weight?
      Is mine better than his?
      How are you today?
        But do you actually have the hours available
      Or the interest - or empathy
      For me to express to you
      How I really am?

Every day many dive into a trivial sea
  Of innumerable shallow pursuits
    And foolish quests
      Not cognizant of a question's innate yearning
    Its natural longing to steer us
      Up the narrow mountain path
        Where only from a triumphant crest
      Can one achieve remembrance
        Of the ever-rumbling inquiries

"Who am I?"
  "Why am I here?
    "What is my true purpose?"
      "What is the meaning of my life?"
        The ones sincere adventurers shout
          From the serene peaks of mountains

Yet even the question
  "Do I need a better toothbrush?"
    Leads to brushing my molars and bicuspids
      So I can maintain healthy teeth
        In order to chew food well
          So I can nourish my body
            In order to survive and thrive
              So I can develop the energy
                And take the essential time
                  To one day ask myself - "Who am I?"

These intimate examinations
  The ones requiring no solid answers
    Are like captains of wintry icebreaker ships
      Cracking open northern routes
        Through stratums of frozen oceans
          Where vessels could not journey before

Like ardent space travelers
  Exploring the edgeless threshold
    Of all that is possible

Like heroic pioneers charting unmapped territory
  Or archeologists cutting through lush thick jungles
    Where there are no footprints

To these audacious adventurers
  Who ache for a glimpse of the sublime
    The answers are porous - malleable - ever changing
      Yet the questions are solid as a rock

## The Great Circle Mantra

My life is unfolding perfectly
Just the way it is
Because all that truly exists
Is *Perfect Love*
Yet I am here
To help the world become more perfect
By living my life
Perfectly guided by *Love*

# ✳ WHAT IS – JOURNEY OF THE GREAT CIRCLE ✳

JOURNEY OF THE GREAT CIRCLE is a collection of 365 contemplative narratives designed as a daily transformative practice for the purpose of personal transformation. The annual collection of narratives is divided into four volumes, Winter, Spring, Summer, and Autumn each beginning on either the solstice or equinox. Each of the 365 narratives has a specific spiritual theme to help you gain a more expansive understanding of what really matters - and points you to how to live a life with peace of mind and inner freedom.

The various themes of the narratives involve insights from spirituality, quantum physics, the evolutionary perspective, the study of visionary archetypes, healing, and transformative practice. **Journey of The Great Circle** can be thought of as "a spiritual map of an awakening life".

A life of inner freedom is when one consciously realizes the perfection that's always unfolding within - and within all of life. Living with this awareness allows the natural states of peace, happiness, joy and harmony to effortlessly arise. It is a life of one who has devotedly learned to love others and all of life unconditionally - and who has gained the joyful awareness of serving the wellbeing of others. In these writings, one who attains this level of mastery is referred to as a **Master of Freedom**.

We are all natural-born storytellers with a mandate from *Life* to generate the most fulfilling and creative story of life we can imagine. Every day is a new opportunity to make our life story a little more glorious, a little more fulfilling, a little more creative. We are the authors of this story in every moment of our lives based on the intentions we choose, either consciously or unconsciously. For most people, in order to have the most glorious, fulfilling, creative, and peaceful life requires some form of spiritual practice necessitating conscious attention each day. When **Journey of The Great Circle** is used as a daily practice, it will help cultivate inner freedom - and assist you in fulfilling your sacred destiny of an awakened life as a **Master of Freedom**

The Four Seasonal Volumes of daily Contemplative Practices called
**JOURNEY OF THE GREAT CIRCLE**     by Oman Ken
can be acquired through:     balboapress.com
and other prominent bookstores

# JOURNEY OF *THE GREAT CIRCLE*

| | |
|---|---|
| Winter Volume: | December 21 – March 18 |
| Spring Volume: | March 19 – June 19 |
| Summer Volume: | June 20 – September 21 |
| Autumn Volume: | September 22 – December 20 |

The 17 Contemplative Circles which are displayed before some of the poems in this book are excerpts from Oman Ken's visionary book – **Journey of *The Great Circle***.

✳    ✳    ✳    ✳

# ✳ ABOUT THE AUTHOR ✳

OMAN KEN HAS DEVOTED HIS LIFE to being a multi-instrumentalist, vocalist, writer, and poet. He lives in a home filled with exotic instruments from around the world, and professionally has focused his musical presentations on the harp, guitar, piano, Native American and ethnic flutes, as well as the gift of his voice. He has performed hundreds of concerts and celebrations across the United States while creating 15 professional recordings of his original vocal and instrumental music.

Oman has also composed three Ritual Theater Musicals which he directed and produced in Hawaii, entitled "Genesis: A Ritual of Transformation", "Starwheel: Journey of the Sacred Circle", and "The Mask and the Sword". Furthermore, he has produced myriad multi-media Solstice and Equinox Celebrations with a troupe of 25 people in Houston, Texas and Cincinnati, Ohio.

Oman has presented his transformational workshops: "The Ceremonial Art of Celebration", "Dance Movement as Spiritual Practice", and "The Power Within the Archetypes of the King, Warrior, Magician, and Lover", in various spiritual conferences and retreats around the United States.

After a challenging physical condition made it unfeasible to continue his musical travels, Oman deepened his spiritual quest for inner freedom by spending an abundance of time in Nature contemplating what life is truly about - and what really matters.

The result of his personal investigations was a host of poetic contemplative narratives that became his book series **Journey of The Great Circle**. His inquiry also brought forth the 52 story poems in this collection.

Oman now lives in the majestic Red Rocks of Sedona, Arizona.

JourneyOfTheGreatCircle.com

Printed in the United States
by Baker & Taylor Publisher Services